Oh! My Grammar 3

CEDUBOOK

Unit Components

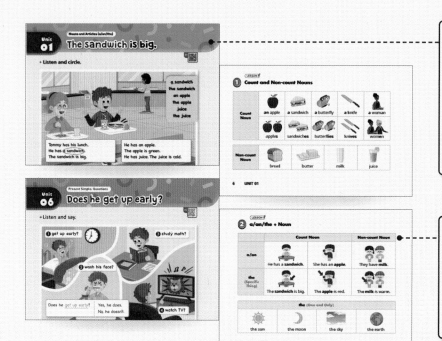

- **LISTEN & CIRCLE**
LISTEN & SAY

Fun and authentic context helps students to easily understand how to use the grammar in real life.

- **GRAMMAR POINT**

Students can learn the target grammar through easy-to-read tables and colorful illustrations with clear examples.

- **LET'S PRACTICE**

Various kinds of exercises and drills are designed to develop students' understanding of the grammar they learned. These will also gradually encourage students to apply the forms accurately.

- **LET'S WRITE**

The extended writing activity encourages students to use the language more productively in a variety of contexts.

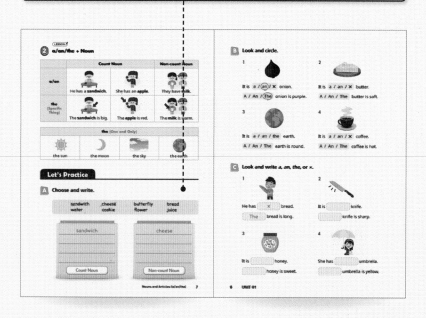

• REVIEW

The review sections help students to recall the language they learned in the previous three to four units. They also allow students to evaluate their understanding of the grammar.

• MINI TEST

The mini test is a cumulative review incorporating the previous seven to eight units. Students will be able to differentiate the grammar points they learned and use them appropriately.

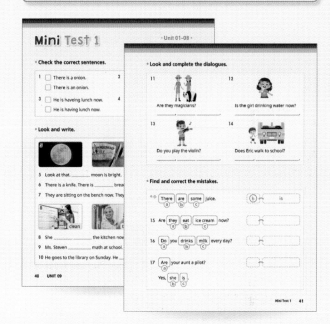

FREE GRAMMAR LESSON

Friendly and detailed grammar audio lessons in Korean are provided to help students comprehend the grammar points more easily.

WORKBOOK

Each unit consists of three steps of writing exercises. These are designed to develop students' sentence building skills. They can reinforce their writing skills and gain confidence by completing the exercises.

Contents

Nouns & Be Verbs

Present Simple & Present Continuous

Imperatives & Future Tense

Past Tense

Wh- Questions & Others

Nouns and Articles (a/an/the)

The sandwich is big.

✦ **Listen and circle.**

a sandwich
the sandwich
an apple
the apple
juice
the juice

Tommy has his lunch.
He has a sandwich.
The sandwich is big.

He has an apple.
The apple is green.
He has juice. The juice is cold.

1 **Count and Non-count Nouns**

Count Noun	**an** apple	**a** sandwich	**a** butterfly	**a** knife	**a** woman
	apple**s**	sandwich**es**	butterfl**ies**	kni**ves**	wom**en**

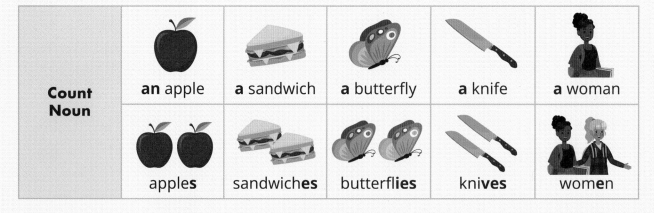

Non-count Noun	bread	butter	milk	juice

LESSON 2 a/an/the + Noun

	Count Noun		Non-count Noun
a/an	He has **a sandwich**.	She has **an apple**.	They have **milk**.
the (Specific Thing)	**The sandwich** is big.	**The apple** is red.	**The milk** is warm.

the (One and Only)			
the sun	**the** moon	**the** sky	**the** earth

Let's Practice

A Choose and write.

sandwich	~~cheese~~	butterfly	bread
water	cookie	flower	juice

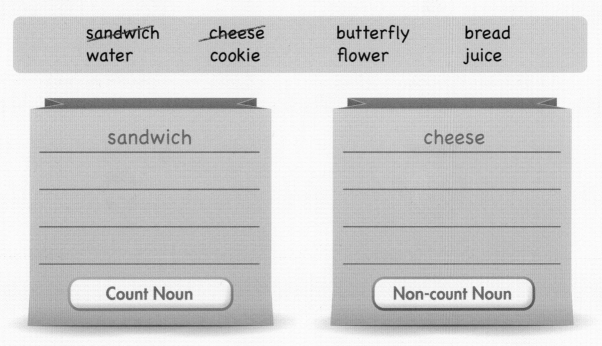

sandwich

_____

_____

_____

Count Noun

cheese

_____

_____

_____

Non-count Noun

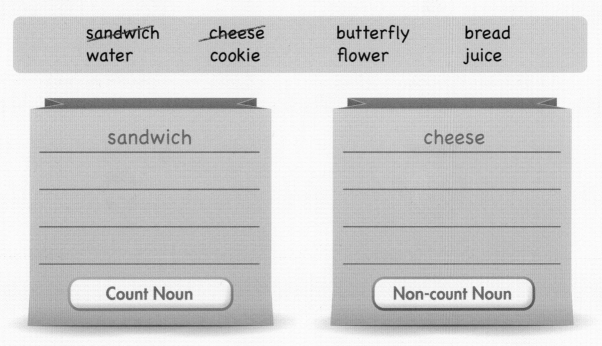

B Look and circle.

1

It is   a / (an) / ✕   onion.

A / An / (The)   onion is purple.

2

It is   a / an / ✕   butter.

A / An / The   butter is soft.

3

It is   a / an / the   earth.

A / An / The   earth is round.

4

It is   a / an / ✕   coffee.

A / An / The   coffee is hot.

C Look and write *a*, *an*, *the,* or *x*.

1

He has [✕] bread.

[The] bread is long.

2

It is [   ] knife.

[   ] knife is sharp.

3

It is [   ] honey.

[   ] honey is sweet.

4

She has [   ] umbrella.

[   ] umbrella is yellow.

Let's Write

✏ **Look, choose, and complete the sentences.**

Ben's   Mia's

~~orange~~   cookie   soup   juice   bread   hamburger

① Ben has   an   orange   .   The   orange   is round.

② Ben has   .   is soft.

③ Ben has   .   is hot.

④ Mia has   .   is cold.

⑤ Mia has   .   is big.

⑥ Mia has   .   is sweet.

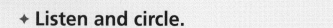

Unit 02

They are vets.

✦ **Listen and circle.**

he is
she is
they are
they are not
it is
it is not

He is James. She is Emily.
They are vets.
They are not zookeepers.

There are penguins.
One penguin is old.
It is sick. It is not okay.

LESSON ✎

① **Be Verb: Positives and Negatives**

	Positive	Negative
I	am	am not (= I'm not)
You	are	are not (= aren't)
He / She / It	is	is not (= isn't)
We / You / They	are	are not (= aren't)

Kate **is** a zookeeper.
Kate **isn't** a pilot.

Tim and Amy **are** young.
They **aren't** old.

It **is** a penguin.
It **isn't** an owl.

Be Verb: Questions

Question	Answer	
Are you ...?	Yes, I **am**.	No, **I'm not**.
Is he / she / it ...?	Yes, he / she / it **is**.	No, he / she / it **isn't**.
Are you / we / they ...?	Yes, we / you / they **are**.	No, we / you / they **aren't**.

Is Steve a pilot?
Yes, he **is**.

Are the children bored?
No, they **aren't**.
They're excited.

Are the penguins big?
No, they **aren't**.
They're small.

Let's Practice

A Look, choose, and write.

①  ②  ③ 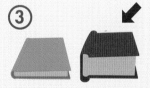 ④

| is | are | isn't | aren't |

1 Ian _____is_____ a tennis player. He _____isn't_____ a baseball player.

2 The apples _____ green. They _____ red.

3 The orange book _____ thick. It _____ thin.

4 Kate and Leo _____ police officers. They _____ firefighters.

B Look, write, and circle.

1 __Is__ __it__ old?

   (Yes, it is.) / No, it isn't.

2 _____ _____ a pilot?

   Yes, I am. / No, I'm not.

3 _____ _____ a nurse?

   Yes, she is. / No, she isn't.

4 _____ _____ cold?

   Yes, they are. / No, they aren't.

C Look and write.

1 The girl [is] angry. She [isn't] happy.

2 The cheetahs [ ] fast. They [ ] slow.

3 My sister and I [ ] excited. We [ ] bored.

4 [ ] the man a singer? No, [ ] [ ].

5 [ ] Lina an artist? Yes, [ ] [ ].

6 [ ] the mittens yellow? No, [ ] [ ].

Let's Write

✎ **Look and complete the dialogues.**

Sally

Anna and Sean

① **Q** [Is] Sally a zookeeper?

A [Yes] , [she] [is] .

② **Q** [   ] the pandas hungry?

A [   ] , [   ] [   ] .

③ **Q** [   ] the hospital old?

A [   ] , [   ] [   ] . It [   ] new.

④ **Q** [   ] Anna and Sean bakers?

A [   ] , [   ] [   ] . They [   ] dentists.

Unit 03

There + Be + Noun

There is some cheese.

✦ Listen and circle.

there is a
there is an
there are some
there is some
there is some

There is a potato.
There is an onion.
There are some carrots.

There is some cheese.
There is some salt.
We can make soup for dinner.

LESSON

1 There + Be + Count Noun

There is + Singular Noun	There are + (some) + Plural Noun
There is a carrot.	**There are (some)** carrots.
There is an onion.	**There are (some)** onions.

2 There + Be + Non-count Noun

There is + (some) + Non-count Noun	
There is (some) soup.	There is (some) cheese.
There is (some) water.	There is (some) salt.

Let's Practice

A Look and circle.

1 There is / **are** some carrots.

2 There is / are a tomato.

3 There is / are some soup.

4 There is / are some cups.

5 There is / are some sugar.

6 There is / are some grapes.

B Read and write *a*, *an*, or *some*.

1 There is ___some___ cheese.

2 There is _____ water.

3 There is _____ onion.

4 There is _____ salt.

5 There are _____ forks.

6 There is _____ potato.

C Look, circle, and write.

1 There [is] [a] spoon.
(is) / are   (a) / some

2 There [   ] [   ] milk.
is / are   a / some

3 There [   ] [   ] eggs.
is / are   an / some

4 There [   ] [   ] orange.
is / are   an / some

5 There [   ] [   ] rice.
is / are   a / some

Let's Write

✎ **Spot the differences between the two pictures.**
Then, complete the sentences with *a*, *an*, or *some*.

Picture A

Picture B

① In ⌈Picture A⌋,　there　is　a　strawberry.
In ⌈Picture B⌋,　there　are　some　strawberries.

② In ⌈Picture A⌋,　　　　　　　　　　　sandwiches.
In ⌈Picture B⌋,　　　　　　　　　　　sandwich.

③ In ⌈Picture A⌋,　　　　　　　　　　　ice cream.
In ⌈Picture B⌋,　　　　　　　　　　　cookies.

④ In ⌈Picture A⌋,　　　　　　　　　　　apple.
In ⌈Picture B⌋,　　　　　　　　　　　apple jam.

Review 1

A Check the correct sentences.

1
☐ She has a orange.
☑ She has an orange.

2
☐ There is a fork.
☐ There is forks.

3
☐ The kids have a bread.
☐ The kids have bread.

4
☐ There is some salt.
☐ There are some salt.

5
☐ There is some lemons.
☐ There are some lemons.

6
☐ An earth is beautiful.
☐ The earth is beautiful.

B Look and write *a*, *an*, *the*, or *some*.

1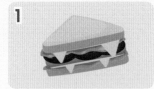
2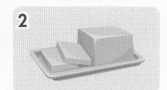
3

1 There is _____a_____ sandwich.

2 There is _____ butter.

3 There are _____ carrots.

4
5
6

4 It is _____ sun. _____ sun is hot.

5 Sally has _____ umbrella. _____ umbrella is yellow.

6 It is _____ knife. _____ knife is sharp.

C Look, choose, and write.

| isn't | am | are | is | aren't | isn't |

1

Amy ____isn't____ a doctor.

2

There _____ some grapes.

3

There _____ some soup.

4

I _____ a tennis player.

5

The book _____ thin.

6

The kids _____ excited.

D Read and complete the dialogues.

1 Q ___Is___ your sister tall?

A Yes, ___she___ ___is___.

2 Q _____ they artists?

A Yes, _____ _____.

3 Q _____ the shoes new?

A No, _____ _____.

4 Q _____ your puppy sick?

A No, _____ _____.

E **Look and write.**

1

There _____ a butterfly. *is*

2

It is _____ spoon.

3

I _____ a doctor.
I'm not a scientist.

4

We're teachers.
We _____ students.

5

There is some milk.
There _____ some cookies.

6

There is an egg.
There is _____ cheese.

7

Tim has _____ onion.
_____ onion is purple.

8

Look at the sky.
_____ moon is big.

9

_____ the boy angry?
Yes, _____ _____.

10

_____ they tigers?
No, _____ _____.

F **Correct the mistakes.**

1 He has a <u>juice</u>. → [some] juice

2 My aunt <u>aren't</u> a cook. →

3 I have <u>a</u> orange. →

4 There <u>are</u> some sugar. →

5 There are stars in <u>a</u> sky. →

6 There is a <u>jam</u>. →

7 The mice <u>is</u> small. →

8 <u>Are</u> your dad a police officer? →

Unit 05
Mia studies English.

+ **Listen and circle.**

walk ~~walk~~
doesn't walk
studies
don't study

I walk to school in the morning.
Mia doesn't walk to school.
She takes a bus.

Mia and I study in the afternoon.
Mia studies English.
I don't study English. I study math.

 LESSON

1 Present Simple: Positives and Negatives

Positive	Negative
I / You / We / They **drink** milk.	I / You / We / They **don't drink** milk.
He / She / It **drinks** milk.	He / She / It **doesn't drink** milk.

I **get up** at 6 o'clock.
I **don't get up** at 7 o'clock.

She **has** breakfast at 7 o'clock.
She **doesn't have** breakfast at 8 o'clock.

Regular and Irregular Verbs

Regular Verbs			Irregular Verbs
-s	**-es**	**-ies**	
walk – walk**s** like – like**s** clean – clean**s**	bru**sh** – brush**es** cat**ch** – catch**es** pas**s** – pass**es** mi**x** – mix**es**	stud**y** – stud**ies** fl**y** – fl**ies** carr**y** – carr**ies** tr**y** – tr**ies**	have – **has**
pl**ay** – play**s**	d**o** – do**es**		

I **brush** my hair in the morning.
He **brushes** his teeth in the morning.

I **study** English in the evening.
He **studies** math in the evening.

I **don't like** carrots.
Mina **doesn't like** beans.

I **don't drink** soda.
Mina **doesn't drink** milk.

Let's Practice

A **Read and circle.**

1 I (get up) / gets up early every day.

2 The man carry / carries a box.

3 My dad don't / doesn't like coffee.

4 Nate and I take / takes a bus every day.

5 The kids don't / doesn't watch TV at night.

B **Read and write the correct forms of the verbs.**

1 study

The students __study__ math.

They __don't__ __study__ science.
[not]

2 have

My aunt _____ a kitten.

She _____ _____ a puppy.
[not]

3 like

Amy and I _____ oranges.

We _____ _____ kiwis.
[not]

4 brush

Leo _____ his teeth.

He _____ _____ his hair.
[not]

C **Look, choose, and write.**

drink	fly	walk	mix

The children __drink__ milk.

They __don't__ __drink__ soda.

She _____ a kite in summer.

She _____ _____ a kite in winter.

The cook _____ eggs.

He _____ _____ cream.

They _____ the dog in the morning.

They _____ _____ the dog at night.

Let's Write

✎ **Look and complete the sentences.**

	Monday	Wednesday	Friday	Sunday
Helen	go to the library	wash the dog	play baseball	go to the park
Liam	study Korean	play the piano	clean the house	go to the park

① Helen   **goes**   to the library on Monday.

② Liam   Korean on Monday.

③ Helen   the dog on Wednesday.

④ Liam   the flute on Wednesday.

⑤ Helen   basketball on Friday.

⑥ Liam and Helen   to school on Sunday.

Present Simple: Questions

Does he get up early?

✦ **Listen and say.**

❶ get up early?

❷ wash his face?

❸ study math?

❹ watch TV?

| Does he <u>get up early</u>? | Yes, he does. |
| | No, he doesn't. |

LESSON

1 **Present Simple: Do you/we/they ...?**

Question	Answer	
Do you **swim**?	Yes, I / we **do**.	No, I / we **don't**.
Do we **swim**?	Yes, you **do**.	No, you **don't**.
Do they **swim**?	Yes, they **do**.	No, they **don't**.

Do you **get up** at 7:00 every day?
Yes, I **do**.

Do you **go** to school on Sunday?
No, we **don't**.

Present Simple: Does he/she/it ...?

Question	Answer	
Does he **swim**?	Yes, he **does**.	No, he **doesn't**.
Does she **swim**?	Yes, she **does**.	No, she **doesn't**.
Does it **swim**?	Yes, it **does**.	No, it **doesn't**.

Does he **take** a shower every day?
Yes, he **does**.

Does Kate **watch** TV at night?
No, she **doesn't**.

Does Mike **live** in the city?
No, he **doesn't**.

Does a horse **have** a long tail?
Yes, it **does**.

Let's Practice

A **Circle and match.**

1 (Do) / Does they walk to school? ········· Yes, she does.

2 Do / Does Sally have long hair? ········· No, they don't.

3 Do / Does you have breakfast every day? Yes, I do.

B Read and write.

1 ___Does___ he get up early every day?   Yes, ___he___ ___does___.

2 _____ you have lunch at 12:30?   No, _____ _____.

3 _____ she clean her room every day?   No, _____ _____.

4 _____ a pig have a short tail?   Yes, _____ _____.

5 _____ they live in the city?   Yes, _____ _____.

C Look and write.

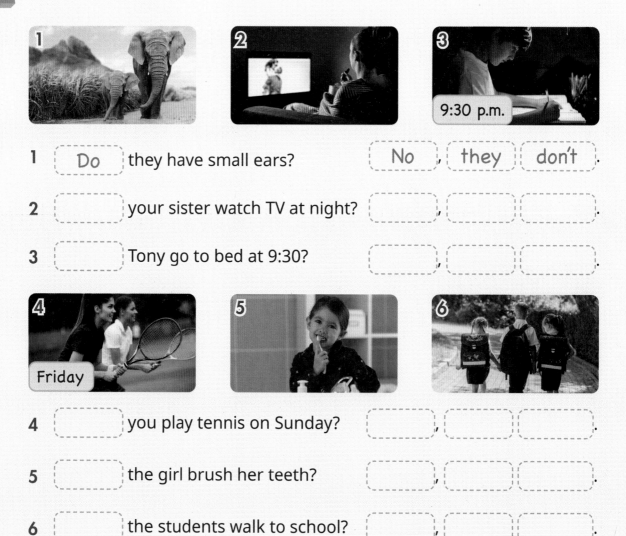

1 (Do) they have small ears?   (No), (they) (don't).

2 ( ) your sister watch TV at night?   ( ), ( ) ( ).

3 ( ) Tony go to bed at 9:30?   ( ), ( ) ( ).

4 ( ) you play tennis on Sunday?   ( ), ( ) ( ).

5 ( ) the girl brush her teeth?   ( ), ( ) ( ).

6 ( ) the students walk to school?   ( ), ( ) ( ).

Let's Write

✏ **Look and complete the dialogues.**

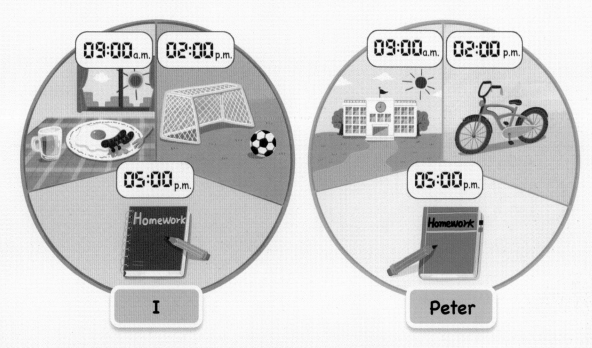

① **Q** [Do] you have breakfast at 9:00?

A [Yes] , [I] [do] .

② **Q** [   ] you play soccer at 1:00?

A [   ] , [   ] [   ] .

③ **Q** [   ] Peter go to school at 10:00?

A [   ] , [   ] [   ] .

④ **Q** [   ] Peter ride his bike at 2:00?

A [   ] , [   ] [   ] .

⑤ **Q** [   ] you and Peter do your homework at 5:00?

A [   ] , [   ] [   ] .

Unit 07

I am riding a bike.

✦ Listen and circle.

am riding
is walking
aren't standing
are sitting

My friends and I are playing
in the park now.
I am riding a bike.

Susie is walking her dog.
Sam and Ted aren't standing.
They are sitting on the bench.

LESSON ✎

1 Present Continuous: Positives

Subject	Be	Verb-ing
I	am	
He / She / It	is	playing.
We / You / They	are	

Verb + -ing		
talk – talking study – studying stand – standing	ride – riding dance – dancing drive – driving	sit – sitting swim – swimming jog – jogging

LESSON

2 Present Continuous: Negatives

Subject	Be + Not	Verb-ing
I	am not (= I'm not)	
He / She / It	is not (= isn't)	playing.
We / You / They	are not (= aren't)	

I **am talking** to my friend now.
I**'m not studying**.

My uncle **is driving** a car now.
He **isn't riding** a bike.

Sandy **is sitting** on a bench now.
She **isn't standing**.

The girls **are jogging** now.
They **aren't walking**.

Let's Practice

 A Read and circle.

1 I (am) / is (eating) / eatting a pizza now.

2 The girl is / are rideing / riding a bike now.

3 They isn't / aren't play / playing a computer game now.

4 My dad isn't / aren't joging / jogging in the park now.

B Read and write.

1 | not / run | They ___aren't___ ___running___ now.

2 | not / cut | Mr. Park _____ _____ the grass now.

3 | make | Amy _____ _____ a sandwich now.

4 | not / wash | We _____ _____ the dishes now.

5 | study | The students _____ _____ math now.

C Look, choose, and write.

| play | drive | sit | swim |

1. They (are) (playing) volleyball now.
They (aren't) (playing) basketball.

2. Amy ( ) ( ) in a pool now.
She ( ) ( ) in the sea.

3. Steve ( ) ( ) a taxi now.
He ( ) ( ) a truck.

4. The dogs ( ) ( ) on a bench now.
They ( ) ( ) on the grass.

Let's Write

✏️ **Look and complete the sentences.**

① **read** — I [am] [reading] a newspaper now.

do — I [am] [not] [doing] my homework.

② **talk** — Kate [ ] [ ] to her friend now.

ride — She [ ] [ ] a scooter.

③ **sit** — The frogs [ ] [ ] on the rock now.

swim — They [ ] [ ] in the pond.

④ **climb** — Thomas [ ] [ ] the tree now.

fly — He [ ] [ ] the kite.

Present Continuous: Questions

Are you studying?

✦ **Listen and circle.**

Are you studying
I'm not
Is your sister writing
she isn't

Sue: Are you studying now?
Josh: No, I'm not.
　　I'm writing a card for Mom.

Sue: Is your sister writing a card, too?
Josh: No, she isn't.
　　She's making a cake.

(LESSON)

1 Present Continuous Question: Singular

Question	Answer	
Are you eat**ing**?	Yes, I **am**.	No, **I'm not**.
Is he / she / it eat**ing**?	Yes, he / she / it **is**.	No, he / she / it **isn't**.

Are you **writing** a letter?
Yes, I **am**.

Is Nate **making** a cake?
No, he **isn't**.
He is making cookies.

2 Present Continuous Question: Plural

Question	Answer	
Are you eat**ing**?	Yes, we **are**.	No, we **aren't**.
Are they eat**ing**?	Yes, they **are**.	No, they **aren't**.

Are you **blowing up** balloons?
Yes, we **are**.

Are they **eating** the cake?
No, they **aren't**.
They are singing a song.

Let's Practice

A Write and match.

1 eat

_____Is_____ the horse _____eating_____ a carrot?   Yes, they are.

2 write

_____ Mary _____ an email?   No, I'm not.

3 study

_____ you _____ English?   Yes, it is.

4 dance

_____ the boy _____?   Yes, she is.

5 sit

_____ people _____ on the bus?   No, he isn't.

B Look and answer the questions.

1	2	3	4

1 Are you listening to music now? ___Yes, I am___.

2 Is Alice blowing up a balloon now? _____.

3 Are they eating the cake now? _____.

4 Is the penguin swimming now? _____.

C Look and write.

1 drive

[Is] the man [driving] the car now?

[No], [he] [isn't].

2 play

[   ] the cats [   ] now?

[   ], [   ] [   ].

3 wash

[   ] Sally [   ] the dog now?

[   ], [   ] [   ].

4 run

[   ] they [   ] on the grass now?

[   ], [   ] [   ].

Let's Write

✏️ **Look and complete the dialogues.**

① **Q** | Is | the magician | holding | the box now? [hold]

   A | Yes | , | he | is | .

② **Q** | | he | | the box now? [close]

   A | | , | | .

   He is opening the box.

③ **Q** | | the birds | | in the box now? [sit]

   A | | , | | .

   The birds are flying out of the box.

④ **Q** | | the people | | now? [laugh]

   A | | , | | .

A Read and circle.

1 He play / (plays) the flute every day.

2 Are they dance / dancing now?

3 The bat flys / flies at night.

4 My sister don't / doesn't get up early.

5 Sam and I isn't / aren't watching TV now.

6 I am cuting / cutting the paper now.

B Look and write the correct forms of the verbs.

get up

He ___gets___ ___up___ early.

He ___doesn't___ ___get___ ___up___ late.

make

I _____ _____ cookies now.

I _____ _____ _____ a cake.

go

We _____ to the park on Sunday.

We _____ _____ to school.

write

Ann _____ _____ a letter now.

She _____ _____ an email.

C Look and complete the dialogues.

jog

_____Do_____ you _____jog_____?

Yes, I do.

swim

_____ she _____ now?

Yes, she is.

_____ he wash his face?

Yes, _____ _____.

_____ you go to bed early?

No, _____ _____.

_____ they taking a bus now?

No, _____ _____.

_____ the monkey climbing now?

Yes, _____ _____.

D Correct the mistakes.

1 A giraffe <u>have</u> a long neck. → has

2 <u>Do</u> your brother exercise every day? →

3 <u>Does</u> she walking the dog now? →

4 The kids are <u>run</u> on the grass now. →

Mini Test 1

◆ **Check the correct sentences.**

1 ☐ There is a onion.

   ☐ There is an onion.

2 ☐ The girl practice soccer.

   ☐ The girl practices soccer.

3 ☐ He is haveing lunch now.

   ☐ He is having lunch now.

4 ☐ There is some honey.

   ☐ There are some honey.

◆ **Look and write.**

sit

5 Look at that. _____ moon is bright.

6 There is a knife. There is _____ bread.

7 They are sitting on the bench now. They _____ _____ on the grass.

clean   teach   go

8 She _____ _____ the kitchen now.

9 Ms. Steven _____ math at school.

10 He goes to the library on Sunday. He _____ _____ to the park.

Look and complete the dialogues.

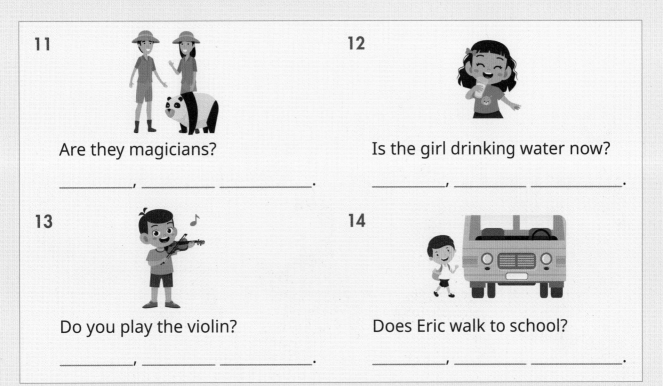

11 Are they magicians?

_____, _____ _____.

12 Is the girl drinking water now?

_____, _____ _____.

13 Do you play the violin?

_____, _____ _____.

14 Does Eric walk to school?

_____, _____ _____.

Find and correct the mistakes.

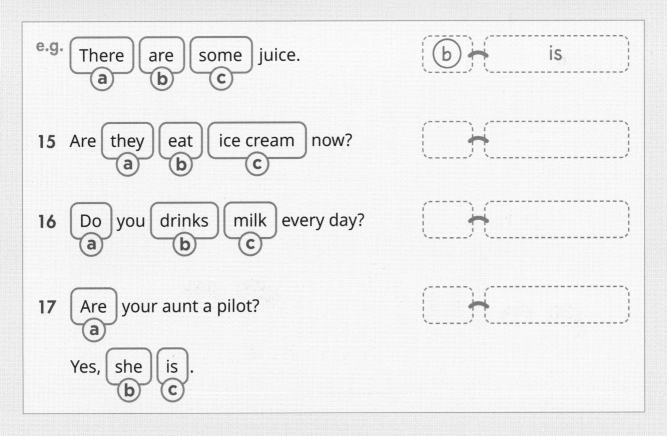

e.g. There (a) are (b) some (c) juice. b ⌢ is

15 Are they (a) eat (b) ice cream (c) now? ⌢

16 Do (a) you drinks (b) milk (c) every day? ⌢

17 Are (a) your aunt a pilot? ⌢

Yes, she (b) is (c).

Let's and Imperatives

Let's go outside.

✦ **Listen and circle.**

> let's go
> let's play
> wear
> don't forget

Kate: Let's go outside.
Jake: Okay. Let's play soccer.
Kate: That sounds great.

Kate's Mom: Kate, it's cold outside.
Wear your jacket.
Don't forget your gloves.

LESSON

1 **Let's**

Positive			Negative		
	go outside.			**go** outside.	
Let's	**play** soccer.		Let's not	**play** soccer.	
	ride a bike.			**ride** a bike.	

It's sunny.
Let's play badminton.

It's rainy.
Let's not go outside.

② Imperatives

Positive	Negative
Run.	**Don't run**.
Open the window.	**Don't open** the window.
Close the door.	**Don't close** the door.

Don't = Do not

Listen to your teacher in class.

Don't run in the library.

It's snowy. **Wear** your gloves.

It's rainy.
Don't forget your umbrella.

Let's Practice

A **Look, circle, and find the correct pictures.**

1 Let's (play) / plays outside.   ⓑ

2 Let's not eats / eat it.

3 Don't sits / sit here.

4 Wear / Wears your scarf.

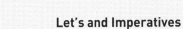

B Choose and write with *Let's* or *Let's not*.

~~buy~~	ride	go	watch	eat

1 It's Mom's birthday. __Let's__ __buy__ some flowers.

2 It's rainy. _____ _____ _____ outside.

3 I'm hungry. _____ _____ a sandwich.

4 It's cold outside. _____ _____ _____ a bike.

5 I'm bored. _____ _____ a movie.

C Look and write.

1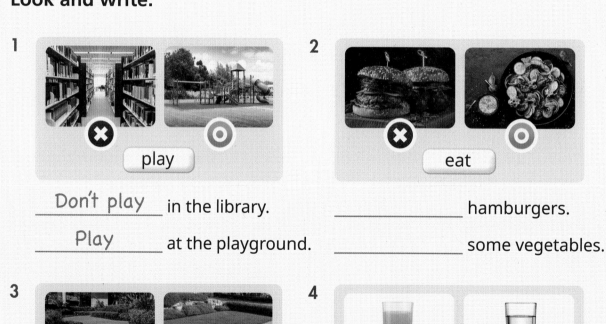

__Don't play__ in the library.

__Play__ at the playground.

2
_____ hamburgers.

_____ some vegetables.

3

_____ on the grass.

_____ on the sidewalk.

4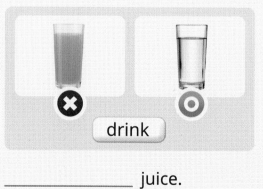

_____ juice.

_____ some water.

Let's Write

✎ **Look, choose, and write the imperatives.**

| sit down | open | talk | draw | use | listen |

Let's follow the rules in the classroom.

①   Sit   down   in class.

②   to your friend in class.

③   your book in class.

④   your phone in class.

⑤   in your book in class.

⑥   to your teacher in class.

Future: Positives and Negatives

I will go to the hospital.

✦ **Listen and circle.**

will go
will not go
will stay
will not go

I'm sick now.
I will go to the hospital tomorrow.
I will not go to school.

My mom is worried about me.
She will stay home with me.
She will not go to work.

LESSON

1 **Future: Positives**

Subject	Will	Verb
I / You / He / They	will (='ll)	go.
It		be sunny.

① 	② 	③ 

① It **will be** rainy tomorrow.

② Liam **will stay** at home.

③ Liam and his dad **will watch** a movie at home.

2 Future: Negatives

Subject	Will + Not	Verb
I / You / He / They	will not (= won't)	go.
It		be sunny.

① It **won't be** rainy tomorrow. It'll be sunny.

② Bella **won't stay** at home. She'll meet her friend.

③ They **won't watch** a movie at home. They'll go to the zoo.

Let's Practice

A Read and circle.

1 Mason is sick. He   will / (won't)   go to school tomorrow.

2 It's cold today. We   will / won't   stay at home.

3 I'm thirsty. I   will / won't   drink some water.

4 The sky is blue. It   will / won't   rain soon.

5 Tim's dog is clean. He   will / won't   wash his dog.

6 My room is dirty. I   will / won't   clean my room tomorrow.

B Look at the to-do list and write.

To-do List for Tomorrow	I	Tom
clean the house	✓	✗
read a book	✓	✓
cook dinner	✗	✓
go shopping	✗	✗

Tomorrow,

1 I ___will___ ___clean___ the house.

2 Tom _____ _____ a book.

3 I _____ _____ dinner.

4 Tom and I _____ _____ shopping.

C Look and write in the future tense.

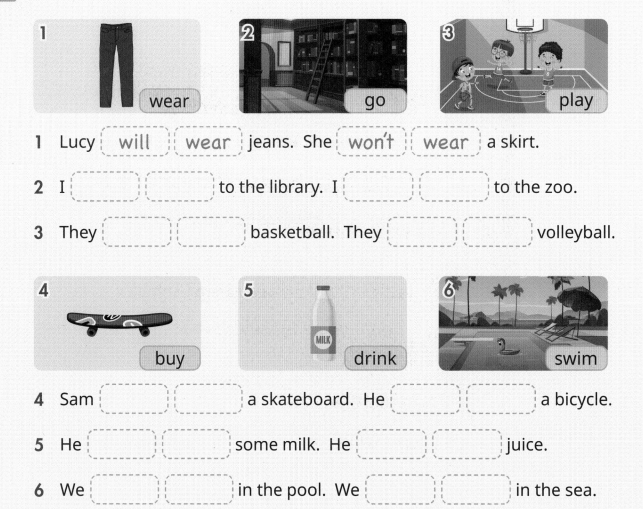

1 wear   2 go   3 play

1 Lucy [will] [wear] jeans. She [won't] [wear] a skirt.

2 I [   ] [   ] to the library. I [   ] [   ] to the zoo.

3 They [   ] [   ] basketball. They [   ] [   ] volleyball.

4 buy   5 drink   6 swim

4 Sam [   ] [   ] a skateboard. He [   ] [   ] a bicycle.

5 He [   ] [   ] some milk. He [   ] [   ] juice.

6 We [   ] [   ] in the pool. We [   ] [   ] in the sea.

Let's Write

✎ **Look, choose, and complete the sentences.**

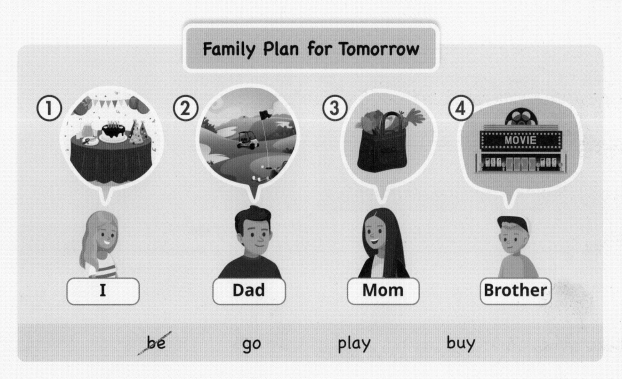

Family Plan for Tomorrow

① I ② Dad ③ Mom ④ Brother

~~be~~ go play buy

This is our family's plan for tomorrow.

① I [will] [be] at my friend's birthday party.

I [won't] [be] at home.

② My dad [   ] [   ] golf.

He [   ] [   ] tennis.

③ My mom [   ] [   ] some vegetables.

She [   ] [   ] ice cream.

④ My brother [   ] [   ] to a movie theater.

He [   ] [   ] to school.

Future: Questions

Will you go swimming?

✦ Listen and say.

❶ visit your grandpa?

❷ go shopping?

❸ go swimming?

❹ climb a mountain?

| Will you visit your grandpa? | Yes, I will. / No, I won't. |

1 Future: Questions

Question			Answer	
Will	you	**go** swimming?	Yes, I / we **will**.	No, I / we **won't**.
	he		Yes, he **will**.	No, he **won't**.
	she		Yes, she **will**.	No, she **won't**.
	we		Yes, you **will**.	No, you **won't**.
	they		Yes, they **will**.	No, they **won't**.
Will	it	**be** rainy?	Yes, it **will**.	No, it **won't**.

Will you **go** on a trip tomorrow?
Yes, I **will**.

Will it **be** rainy tomorrow?
No, it **won't**. It will be sunny.

Will she **take** a train tomorrow?
Yes, she **will**.

Will they **climb** a mountain?
No, they **won't**. They will swim.

Let's Practice

A **Change the sentences to questions.**

1   He will visit his grandma tomorrow.
→ [Will] [he] [visit] his grandma tomorrow?

2   She will clean her room tomorrow.
→ [ ] [ ] [ ] her room tomorrow?

3   They will go to the market tomorrow.
→ [ ] [ ] [ ] to the market tomorrow?

4   He will take a bus tomorrow.
→ [ ] [ ] [ ] a bus tomorrow?

5   It will be cloudy tomorrow.
→ [ ] [ ] [ ] cloudy tomorrow?

B **Write and match.**

1 `come`

_____Will_____ you ___come___ to the party?

2 `take`

_____ Paul _____ an airplane?

3 `stay`

_____ Ann _____ at a hotel?

4 `be`

_____ it _____ sunny tomorrow?

Yes, he will.

No, she won't.

Yes, it will.

No, I won't.

C **Look and write.**

①  go

②  get up

③  wear

1 [Will] [they] [go] to the beach tomorrow?   Yes, they will.

2 [ ] [ ] [ ] [ ] early tomorrow?   Yes, I will.

3 [ ] [ ] [ ] a dress tomorrow?   No, she won't.

④

⑤

⑥

4 Will the kids go camping tomorrow?   [ ] , [ ] [ ] .

5 Will he meet his friend tomorrow?   [ ] , [ ] [ ] .

6 Will you climb a mountain tomorrow?   [ ] , [ ] [ ] .

Let's Write

✎ **Look and complete the dialogues.**

Alex and Lisa have plans tomorrow.

① **Q**   Will   Alex   go   swimming tomorrow?   [go]

  A Yes,   he   will   .

② **Q**   Alex   beach volleyball?   [play]

  A Yes,   .

③ **Q**   Lisa   skiing tomorrow?   [go]

  A No,   .

④ **Q**   Lisa   a coat?   [wear]

  A Yes,   .

⑤ **Q**   Lisa   a scarf?   [bring]

  A No,   .

Future: Questions   53

Review 3

A Check the correct sentences.

1
- [✓] Let's not go shopping.
- [ ] Let's not goes shopping.

2
- [ ] Wear your coat.
- [ ] Wears your coat.

3
- [ ] Mark will ride a bike tomorrow.
- [ ] Mark will rides a bike tomorrow.

4
- [ ] It won't is rainy tomorrow.
- [ ] It won't be rainy tomorrow.

B Look at the to-do lists and write.

Tomorrow's To-do List	
do her homework	✓
wash her dog	✗
meet her friend	✓
watch a movie	✗

Sally

Tomorrow's To-do List	
study English	✓
play tennis	✓
go fishing	✗
watch a movie	✗

Tom

1 Sally ____will____ ____do____ her homework tomorrow.

2 Tom _____ _____ English tomorrow.

3 Sally _____ _____ her dog tomorrow.

4 Will Sally meet her friend tomorrow?

_____, _____ _____.

5 Will Sally and Tom watch a movie tomorrow?

_____, _____ _____.

C Look and write the correct forms of the verbs.

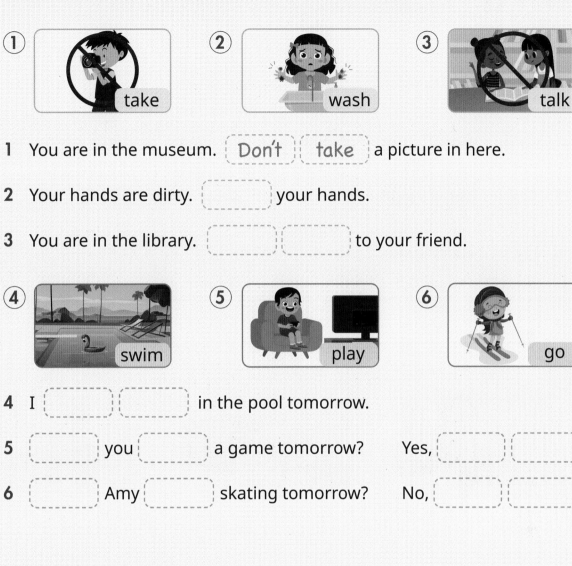

① take ② wash ③ talk

1 You are in the museum. Don't take a picture in here.

2 Your hands are dirty. _____ your hands.

3 You are in the library. _____ _____ to your friend.

④ swim ⑤ play ⑥ go

4 I _____ _____ in the pool tomorrow.

5 _____ you _____ a game tomorrow? Yes, _____ _____ .

6 _____ Amy _____ skating tomorrow? No, _____ _____ .

D Correct the mistakes.

1 He will <u>visits</u> his grandma tomorrow. → visit

2 <u>Doesn't</u> forget your homework. → _____

3 It is sunny. Let's <u>plays</u> outside. → _____

4 I <u>not will</u> get up late tomorrow. → _____

5 <u>Are</u> they go to the zoo tomorrow? → _____

Mini Test 2

◆ **Read and circle.**

1 It   is / will be   cold tomorrow.   2 We   jog / jogging   every day.

3 She is   cooks / cooking   now.   4 Open / Opens   your book.

5 Let's   meet / meets   at 3:00.   6 It   doesn't / won't   rain tomorrow.

◆ **Look and write the correct forms of the verbs.**

brush

drive

wear

7 Sara _____ her teeth every day.

8 He _____ _____ a truck now. He is driving a taxi.

9 I _____ _____ a dress tomorrow.

clean

run

take

10 My sister _____ her room every day.

11 They _____ _____ in the park now.

12 We _____ _____ the school bus tomorrow.

Look and write the correct forms of the verbs.

⑬  practice

⑭ kick

⑮  visit

13 Nate _____ soccer every day.

14 He _____ _____ a ball now.

15 _____ he _____ his friend tomorrow? No, he _____.

⑯  PARK go

⑰  sit

⑱  ride

16 Tom and Susie _____ to the park every day.

17 They _____ _____ now. They are walking.

18 _____ they _____ bikes tomorrow? Yes, they _____.

Find and correct the mistakes.

e.g. We | don't | watching | TV | every day.
       (a)   (b)   (c)

 (b) → watch

19 The frog | isn't | jumping | now. It's | swim |.
         (a)   (b)   (c)

20 I | don't | stay | home tomorrow. I'll | go | out.
   (a)   (b)   (c)

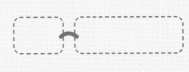

Unit 14

Past: Be Verbs

Amy was at the zoo.

✦ **Listen and circle.**

Yesterday

~~was~~
was
weren't
were
were

It was Children's Day yesterday.
Amy (was) at the zoo.
She was excited.

Ted and Ben weren't at the zoo.
They were at the museum.
They were excited, too.

LESSON ✏

1 **Past Be Verb: Positives and Negatives**

Positive		Negative	
I / He / She / It	**was**	I / He / She / It	**was not** (= **wasn't**)
We / You / They	**were**	We / You / They	**were not** (= **weren't**)

I **was** at the hospital yesterday.
I **wasn't** at home.

They **were** at the museum yesterday.
They **weren't** at school.

Past Be Verb: Questions

Question	Answer	
Were you ...?	Yes, I **was**.	No, I **wasn't**.
Was he / she / it ...?	Yes, he / she / it **was**.	No, he / she / it **wasn't**.
Were you / we / they ...?	Yes, we / you / they **were**.	No, we / you / they **weren't**.

Was it sunny yesterday?
No, it **wasn't**.

Were you bored yesterday?
Yes, I **was**.

Was Tom excited yesterday?
Yes, he **was**.

Was Lina excited yesterday?
No, she **wasn't**.

Let's Practice

 Read and write *was* or *were*.

Today	Yesterday
I am at the library.	1 I ___was___ at the library.
My dog is sick.	2 My dog _____ sick.
They are at the airport.	3 They _____ at the airport.
The weather is nice.	4 The weather _____ nice.
We are at the museum.	5 We _____ at the museum.
My friends are late.	6 My friends _____ late.

B Look and write *was, wasn't, were,* or *weren't.*

1 Lucy __was__ at home yesterday. She __wasn't__ at school.

2 We _____ happy yesterday. We _____ sad.

3 It _____ rainy yesterday. It _____ sunny.

4 They _____ in the classroom. They _____ at the museum.

C Look and write.

1

Was the girl hungry yesterday?

Yes, she was .

2

Mr. Brown tired yesterday?

Yes, .

3

you at the library yesterday?

No, .

4

the children at the zoo yesterday?

No, .

✏ **Look and complete the sentences.**

Yesterday

Cindy

Daniel and Erin

① Cindy   was   at the movie theater yesterday.

She   wasn't   at home.

② Q   the movie sad?

A No,   . It   funny.

③ Daniel and Erin   at the swimming pool yesterday.

They   at school.

④ Q   the weather hot?

A Yes,   .

⑤ Q   Daniel and Erin bored?

A No,   . They   excited.

Unit 15

Past: Regular Verbs

I watched a concert.

✦ Listen and circle.

watched
danced
jumped
didn't dance
didn't jump
didn't like

Lily and I (watched) a concert yesterday.
Lily danced.
She jumped.

But I didn't dance.
I didn't jump.
I didn't like the concert.

1 Past: Positives and Negatives

Positive		Negative	
I / You / We / They	jumped.	I / You / We / They	didn't jump.
He / She / It		He / She / It	

didn't = did not

He **visited** his grandma yesterday.
He **didn't visit** his friend.

We **watched** a soccer game yesterday.
We **didn't watch** a movie.

2 Past Regular Verbs

-ed	-d	-ied
walk – walk**ed** watch – watch**ed** visit – visit**ed**	danc**e** – danced lik**e** – liked bak**e** – baked practic**e** – practiced	cr**y** – cr**ied** stud**y** – stud**ied** carr**y** – carr**ied** tr**y** – tr**ied**
pla**y** – play**ed**		

①    ②    ③

① I **played** at the playground yesterday. I **didn't play** at home.

② Lucas **practiced** the piano yesterday. He **didn't practice** the violin.

③ Eric and Sophia **studied** English yesterday. They **didn't study** Spanish.

Let's Practice

 A Choose and write in the past tense.

walk	dance	bake	study	try
help	carry	like	play	

-ed	-d	-ied
walked		

B Look, choose, and write.

①  ②  ③  ④

| ~~cook~~ | play | dance | carry |

1 My brother and I ___cooked___ dinner yesterday.

2 The kids _____ to the music yesterday.

3 Steve and Noah _____ a basket together yesterday.

4 My sister _____ the violin yesterday.

C Look and write in the past tense.

bake

Grandma and I [baked] a pie yesterday.

We [didn't] [bake] cupcakes.

study

Nate [_____] math yesterday.

He [_____] [_____] science.

wash

My aunt [_____] her car yesterday.

She [_____] [_____] her bicycle.

live

Adam and Mary [_____] in a house.

They [_____] [_____] in an apartment.

Let's Write

✎ **Look and complete the sentences.**

Yesterday,

① Mike ⬜visited⬜ his friend.

Kelly ⬜didn't⬜ ⬜visit⬜ her uncle.

② Mike ⬜⬜⬜ ⬜⬜⬜ taekwondo.

Kelly ⬜⬜⬜ yoga.

③ Mike ⬜⬜⬜ volleyball.

Kelly ⬜⬜⬜ ⬜⬜⬜ basketball.

④ Mike and Kelly ⬜⬜⬜ for the math test.

They ⬜⬜⬜ ⬜⬜⬜ for the English test.

Unit 16

Past: Irregular Verbs

I drank soda.

✦ Listen and circle.

went
had
didn't have
drank
didn't drink

Emma and I (went) to a restaurant yesterday.
Emma had salad. I didn't have salad.

I drank soda.
Emma didn't drink soda.
It was a great dinner.

1 Past: Positives and Negatives

Positive		Negative	
I / You / We / They	went.	I / You / We / They	didn't go.
He / She / It		He / She / It	

didn't = did not

He **got up** early yesterday.
He **didn't get up** late.

They **went** on a picnic yesterday.
They **didn't go** fishing.

Past Irregular Verbs

come – c**a**me	do – d**i**d	go – **went**
drink – dr**a**nk	have – h**a**d	eat – **ate**
give – g**a**ve	make – ma**de**	buy – **bought**
write – wr**o**te	see – s**aw**	read – **read**
get – g**o**t	take – t**ook**	cut – **cut**

① Alice **bought** apples yesterday. She **didn't buy** peaches.

② Alice and I **made** an apple pie. We **didn't make** a cake.

③ Alice and I **ate** the pie together. We **didn't eat** cookies.

Let's Practice

 Look and circle.

1

She comed / came to my house yesterday.

2

Mike did / doed his homework yesterday.

3

They have / had a birthday party yesterday.

4

We goed / went on a picnic yesterday.

B **Read and write in the past tense.**

1 | write | I _____wrote_____ an email yesterday.

2 | take | She _____ a shower yesterday.

3 | go | We _____ on a picnic yesterday.

4 | buy | Dad _____ some flowers for Mom.

5 | see | Tom _____ the baseball game yesterday.

6 | have | Kelly and Sam _____ cake yesterday.

C **Look and write.**

1 eat

I [ate] a hamburger yesterday.
I [didn't] [eat] a pizza.

2 drink

They [ ] some juice yesterday.
They [ ] [ ] coffee.

3 read

Kelly [ ] a newspaper yesterday.
She [ ] [ ] a book.

4 make

My brother [ ] a kite yesterday.
He [ ] [ ] a paper airplane.

Let's Write

✏️ **Look and complete the sentences.**

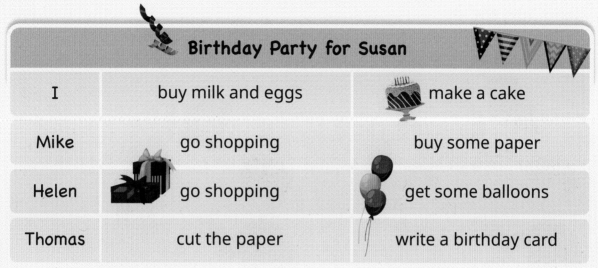

Birthday Party for Susan		
I	buy milk and eggs	make a cake
Mike	go shopping	buy some paper
Helen	go shopping	get some balloons
Thomas	cut the paper	write a birthday card

It was Susan's birthday yesterday. We planned the party.

① I [bought] milk and eggs.

② I _____ a cake.

   I _____ _____ a pie.

③ Mike and Helen _____ shopping together.

④ Helen _____ some balloons.

   She _____ _____ candles.

⑤ Thomas _____ the paper.

⑥ Thomas _____ a birthday card.

   He _____ _____ a letter.

Unit 17

Past: Questions

Did you go to bed late?

✦ Listen and circle.

~~did~~
did
did
didn't

Tim: You look tired.
Did you go to bed late yesterday?
Kelly: Yes, I did.

Tim: Did you do your homework yesterday?
Kelly: No, I didn't. Oh no!

1 Past: Questions

Question			Answer	
Did	you	**go**?	Yes, I / we **did**.	No, I / we **didn't**.
	he / she / it		Yes, he / she / it **did**.	No, he / she / it **didn't**.
	we / they		Yes, you / they **did**.	No, you / they **didn't**.

Did you **go** to school yesterday?
Yes, I **did**.

Did you **walk** to school yesterday?
No, I **didn't**. I took the bus.

Yesterday

① **Did** she **cook** breakfast yesterday?   Yes, she **did**.
② **Did** he **read** a newspaper yesterday?   No, he **didn't**.
③ **Did** they **drink** coffee yesterday?   Yes, they **did**.

Let's Practice

 A **Write and match.**

1 snow

____Did____ it ____snow____ yesterday? · · · · · · ·   No, I didn't.

2 read

_____ you _____ a book?   Yes, it did.

3 study

_____ they _____ for the test?   Yes, she did.

4 go

_____ Anna _____ to school?   No, they didn't.

B Look and answer the questions.

1	2	3	4

1 Did they watch a movie yesterday?   Yes , they   did .

2 Did you eat some chocolate?   ___ , ___   ___ .

3 Did Mike make a cake yesterday?   ___ , ___   ___ .

4 Did Anna play the guitar yesterday?   ___ , ___   ___ .

C Look and write.

Yesterday	do one's homework	clean one's room	take a shower	go to bed early
Leo	O	O	X	X
Sara	O	X	O	O
Noah	X	O	X	O

1 __Did__ Leo __do__ his homework?   Yes, __he__ __did__.

2 _____ Sara _____ her room?   No, _____ _____.

3 _____ Noah _____ a shower?   No, _____ _____.

4 _____ Sara and Noah _____ to bed   Yes, _____ _____.
early?

Let's Write

 Look and complete the dialogues.

My Trip to Seoul	Amy's Trip to Jeju
take the train	go by airplane
visit the N Seoul Tower	climb Halla Mountain
take photos	see dolphins and take photos

I had a great holiday yesterday. Amy did, too.

① **Q** Did you take the train to Seoul?

  A Yes, I did .

② **Q** _____ you visit the amusement park?

  A _____ , _____ _____ .

  I visited the N Seoul Tower.

③ **Q** _____ Amy go by ship?

  A _____ , _____ _____ . She went by airplane.

④ **Q** _____ Amy _____ Halla Mountain?

  A Yes, _____ _____ .

⑤ **Q** _____ you and Amy _____ photos?

  A Yes, _____ _____ .

A Look and circle.

1

I (was) / were at the park yesterday.

I read / readed a book.

2

The students was / were at school yesterday.

They studyed / studied math.

3

My mom was / were at home yesterday.

She maked / made some soup.

4

We was / were on the playground yesterday.

We playd / played soccer.

B Read and match.

1 Did you do your homework yesterday? ⋯⋯⋯⋯ Yes, I did.

2 Was Nancy sick yesterday? No, it didn't.

3 Did it rain yesterday? Yes, they were.

4 Were they at the library yesterday? No, she wasn't.

C Look and write.

①  be

②  be

③  be

1 They [were] at the supermarket yesterday. They [weren't] at home.

2 My brother [   ] tired yesterday. He [   ] okay.

3 We [   ] at the farm yesterday. We [   ] at school.

④  see

⑤  practice

⑥  go

4 She [   ] a giraffe yesterday. She [   ] [   ] a lion.

5 I [   ] taekwondo yesterday. I [   ] [   ] yoga.

6 We [   ] on a picnic yesterday. We [   ] [   ] fishing.

D Read and complete the dialogues.

1 Did you help your mom yesterday?   Yes, [I] [did].

2 Did Lina write a letter yesterday?   No, [   ] [   ].

3 Were they at the museum yesterday?   No, [   ] [   ].

4 [   ] the weather hot yesterday?   Yes, [   ] was.

5 [   ] he walk to school yesterday?   Yes, [   ] did.

Mini Test 3

◆ **Check the correct sentences.**

1 ☐ He will see a doctor.
☐ He will sees a doctor.

2 ☐ We aren't at home yesterday.
☐ We weren't at home yesterday.

3 ☐ The baby cryed loudly.
☐ The baby cried loudly.

4 ☐ I won't go camping tomorrow.
☐ I didn't go camping tomorrow.

◆ **Look and write the correct forms of the verbs.**

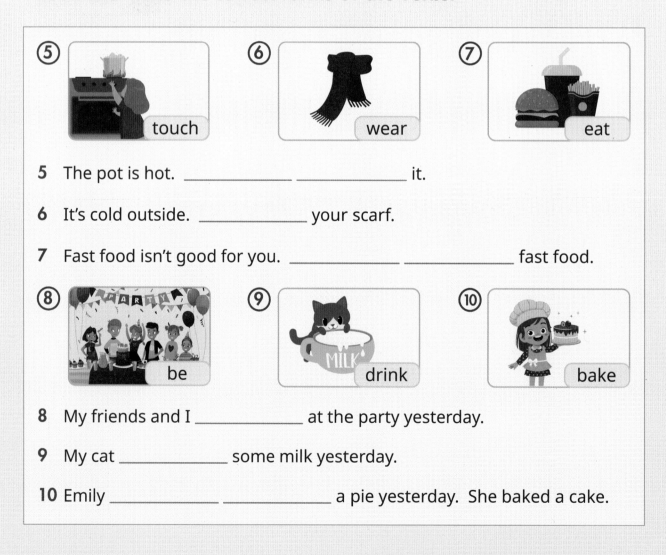

⑤ touch   ⑥ wear   ⑦ eat

5 The pot is hot. _____ _____ it.

6 It's cold outside. _____ your scarf.

7 Fast food isn't good for you. _____ _____ fast food.

⑧ be   ⑨ drink   ⑩ bake

8 My friends and I _____ at the party yesterday.

9 My cat _____ some milk yesterday.

10 Emily _____ _____ a pie yesterday. She baked a cake.

♦ **Look and write the correct forms of the verbs.**

⑪  be

⑫  be

⑬  wash

11 _____ you sick yesterday?   Yes, I _____.

12 _____ your dad at home yesterday?   No, he _____.

13 _____ he _____ the dishes yesterday?   Yes, he _____.

⑭  buy

⑮  do

⑯ ride

14 _____ they _____ some oranges tomorrow?   No, they _____.

15 _____ she _____ her homework tomorrow?   Yes, she _____.

16 _____ you _____ a bike tomorrow?   No, I _____.

♦ **Find and correct the mistakes.**

e.g. I | didn't | played | yesterday. I | studied |.
        (a)   (b)   (c)

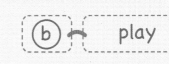 (b) ⤙ play

17 We | don't | eat | cookies | yesterday.
       (a)   (b)   (c)

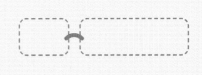

18 It | will | is | cold tomorrow.
      (a) (b)

| Don't | go outside.
   (c)

Unit 19

Wh- Questions

Where were you?

✦ **Listen and circle.**

what
where
who

Grandma asks Noah.
"Noah, (what) are they?"
"They are my photos."

"Where were you?"
"I was in the park."
"Who is he?" "He is my friend, Andy."

 LESSON

1 What and Who

	Present	Past
What (Things)	Q: **What** is it? A: It is **a photo**.	Q: **What** was it? A: It was **a bird**.
Who (People)	Q: **Who** are they? A: They are **actors**.	Q: **Who** were they? A: They were **my classmates**.

Who is he?
He is **a photographer**.

What are they?
They are **his cameras**.

Whose

	Present	Past
Whose (Possessions)	Q: **Whose** *ring* is it? A: It is **my sister's ring**.	Q: **Whose** *cap* was it? A: It was **Steve's cap**.

Mr. Lee

Whose *glasses* are they?
They are **Mr. Lee's glasses**.

Megan

Whose *scarf* was it?
It was **Megan's scarf**.

Where and When

	Present	Past
Where (Places)	Q: **Where** are the students? A: They are **in the library**.	Q: **Where** was the backpack? A: It was **under the bed**.
When (Time)	Q: **When** is the picnic? A: It is **in March**. It is **on Thursday**.	Q: **When** was the class? A: It was **at 9 o'clock**.

Where is the cup?
It is **on the table**.

Where are the cookies?
They are **in the jar**.

Mon | Test 3:00
Tue | Today
Wed | Piano lesson

When was the test?
It was **at 3 o'clock**.

When is the piano lesson?
It is **on Wednesday**.

Let's Practice

A Look, choose, and write.

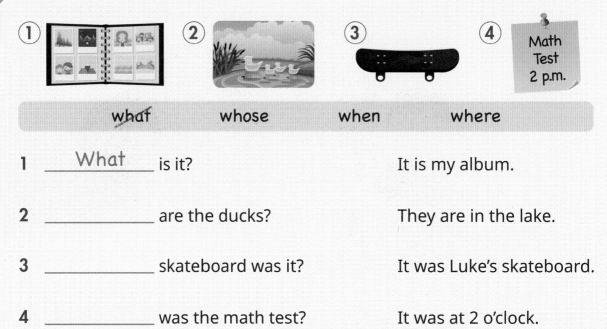

① ② ③ ④ Math Test 2 p.m.

| ~~what~~ | whose | when | where |

1 _____What_____ is it?   It is my album.

2 _____ are the ducks?   They are in the lake.

3 _____ skateboard was it?   It was Luke's skateboard.

4 _____ was the math test?   It was at 2 o'clock.

B Look and write.

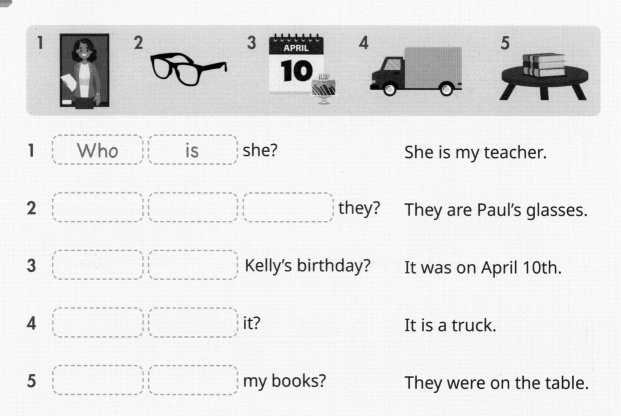

1 [Who] [is] she?   She is my teacher.

2 [   ] [   ] [   ] they?   They are Paul's glasses.

3 [   ] [   ] Kelly's birthday?   It was on April 10th.

4 [   ] [   ] it?   It is a truck.

5 [   ] [   ] my books?   They were on the table.

✏️ **Look, choose, and complete the dialogues.**

① **May 5th**

when   what   whose   who   where

① **Q** [When] [was] the barbecue party?
A It was on May 5th.

② **Q** [   ] [   ] [   ] it?
A It is Andrew's hat.

③ **Q** [   ] [   ] they?
A They are hot dogs.

④ **Q** [   ] [   ] the cat?
A It is under the table.

⑤ **Q** [   ] [   ] the children?
A They are Andrew's friends.

Adjectives and Adverbs

She speaks quietly.

✦ **Listen and circle.**

shy
quietly
loudly
kind
good

Diana is a (shy) girl.
She speaks quietly.
She doesn't speak loudly.

But she is kind.
She is a good friend.
Everyone likes her.

 LESSON 🖊

1 Adjectives

Be + Adjective	Be + (a/an) + Adjective + Noun
The turtle **is slow**.	It **is** a **slow turtle**.
The cars **are fast**.	They **are fast cars**.

LESSON 🖊

2 Adverbs

Verb + Adverb	
The man **drives slowly**.	The children **speak quietly**.
The man **drives fast**.	The children **speak loudly**.

More Adjectives and Adverbs

quiet → quiet**ly**	slow → slow**ly**	fast → **fast**
loud → loud**ly**	kind → kind**ly**	early → **early**
careful → careful**ly**	happy → happ**ily**	late → **late**
dangerous → dangerous**ly**	noisy → nois**ily**	good → **well**

She is **fast**. She is a **fast** runner.
She runs **fast**.

He is **slow**. He is a **slow** walker.
He walks **slowly**.

Brian is a **good** soccer player.
He plays soccer **well**.

My mom is a **careful** driver.
She drives the car **carefully**.

Let's Practice

 Read and circle.

1 She is a (slow) / slowly walker.   2 The baby sleeps quiet / quietly .

3 I got up early / earlily .   4 He is running fast / fastly .

5 The kids are noisy / noisily .   6 Sue is a happy / happily girl.

B Read and write the *adjectives* or *adverbs*.

1 The boy is [loud]. He speaks <u>loudly</u>.

2 Sarah is a <u>careful</u> girl. She carries the box [   ].

3 Oliver and Daisy are <u>quiet</u>. They talk [   ].

4 My brother is a [   ] reader. He reads books <u>slowly</u>.

5 They are [   ] baseball players. They play baseball <u>well</u>.

C Look and write the *adjectives* and *adverbs*.

①   ②   ③

1 [noisy] The dog is [noisy]. The dog barks [noisily].

2 [good] She is a [   ] artist. She paints [   ].

3 [late] Tim was [   ]. He went to school [   ].

④   ⑤   ⑥

4 [fast] The swimmer is [   ]. He swims [   ].

5 [happy] They are [   ]. They are laughing [   ].

6 [kind] He is a [   ] boy. He helps an old lady [   ].

Let's Write

✎ **Look, choose, and write with the given verbs.**

happy	careful	slow	good

① Ms. Green is a ___happy___ teacher.

She ___smiles___ ___happily___ .

　　　[smile]

② My father is a _____ cook.

He _____ _____ .

　　　[cook]

③ The man is a _____ driver.

He _____ the car _____ .

　　　[drive]

④ A snail is a _____ animal.

It _____ _____ .

　　　[move]

Comparatives

The car is faster than the bike.

17

✦ **Listen and circle.**

lighter than
faster than
bigger than

Chris has a bike, a car, and a truck.
The bike is (lighter than) the car.

The car is faster than the bike.
The truck is bigger than the car.
Which one will he take today?

LESSON

1 **Adjective + -er + than**

| A train is | **faster than** | a car. |

LESSON

2 **Comparative: -er and -r**

| + -er | small – small**er**
light – light**er** | + -r | larg**e** – large**r**
nic**e** – nice**r** |

Japan   China

Japan is **smaller than** China.

Russia   China

Russia is **larger than** China.

3 Comparative: *-er*, *-ier*, and *more* +

double consonant + -er	bi**g** – big**ger** ho**t** – hot**ter**	+ -ier	heav**y** – heav**ier** eas**y** – eas**ier**
more +		expensive – **more** expensive dangerous – **more** dangerous	

The earth is **bigger than** the moon.   The hippo is **heavier than** the zebra.

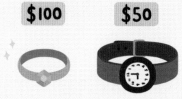

The tiger is **more dangerous than** the fox.   The ring is **more expensive than** the watch.

Let's Practice

 Write the comparative adjectives.

1 fast → *faster*   2 hot →

3 heavy →   4 beautiful →

5 large →   6 small →

7 big →   8 nice →

B Read and write.

1 small ···· Seoul is _smaller_ _than_ Tokyo.

2 hot ···· India is _____ _____ Canada in summer.

3 nice ···· The blue bike is _____ _____ the green bike.

4 easy ···· This puzzle is _____ _____ that puzzle.

C Look, circle, and write.

①
slow / fast

1 A bus is _slower_ _than_ an airplane.

2 The sun is _____ _____ the earth.

②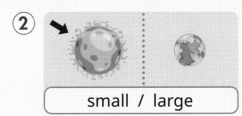
small / large

③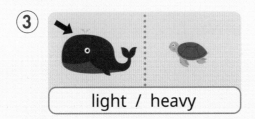
light / heavy

3 The whale is _____ _____ the turtle.

4 A watermelon is _____ _____ _____ an apple.

④
cheap / expensive

⑤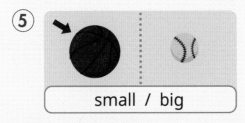
small / big

5 A basketball is _____ _____ a baseball.

6 The fox's tail is _____ _____ the rabbit's tail.

⑥
short / long

Let's Write

✎ **Look and complete the sentences.**

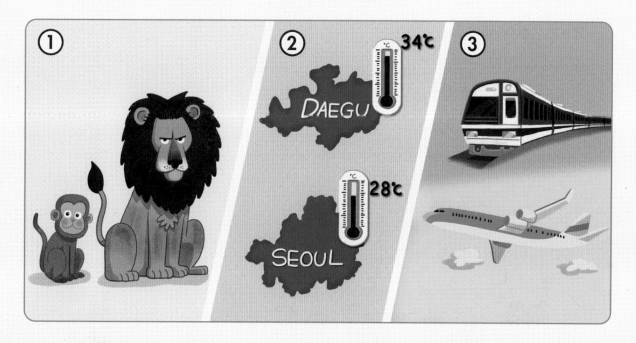

① **small** The monkey is smaller than the lion.

large The lion is ☐ ☐ the monkey.

dangerous The lion is ☐ ☐ ☐ the monkey.

② **hot** Daegu is ☐ ☐ Seoul.

cool Seoul is ☐ ☐ Daegu.

③ **slow** A train is ☐ ☐ an airplane.

fast An airplane is ☐ ☐ a train.

A Read and circle.

1 The man speaks ~~quiet~~ / (quietly).

2 She is a good / well pianist.

3 The music was loud / loudly.

4 The baby is crying noisy / noisily.

B Look, circle, and write.

①   ②    ③

1 good / (well)   The boy plays the basketball   well   .

2 happy / happily   They are   children.

3 careful / carefully   They listen to the teacher   .

④    ⑤    ⑥

4 When / Where   the party?
It was on Sunday.

5 Where / What   the gifts?
They are under the Christmas tree.

6 Who / Whose   scarf   it?
It was Andrew's scarf.

C Look, choose, and write.

| ~~fast~~ | large | expensive | heavy |

1

A car is ___faster___ ___than___
a bicycle.

2

A stone is _____ _____
a feather.

3

A ship is _____ _____
a boat.

4

The dress is _____ _____
_____ the skirt.

D Correct the mistakes.

1 These are <u>beautifully</u> flowers. → beautiful

2 He drives a car <u>fastly</u>. →

3 India is <u>hoter</u> than Korea. →

4 Q Whose rain boots are they?
A <u>It is</u> Sophie's rain boots. →

5 Q <u>What</u> was she?
A She was Brian's sister. →

Mini Test 4

◆ **Check the correct sentences.**

1 ☐ I am at the theater yesterday. 2 ☐ Thomas ate cake.

   ☐ I was at the theater yesterday.   ☐ Thomas eated cake.

3 ☐ China is biger than Japan. 4 ☐ The library was quiet.

   ☐ China is bigger than Japan.   ☐ The library was quietly.

◆ **Look and write.**

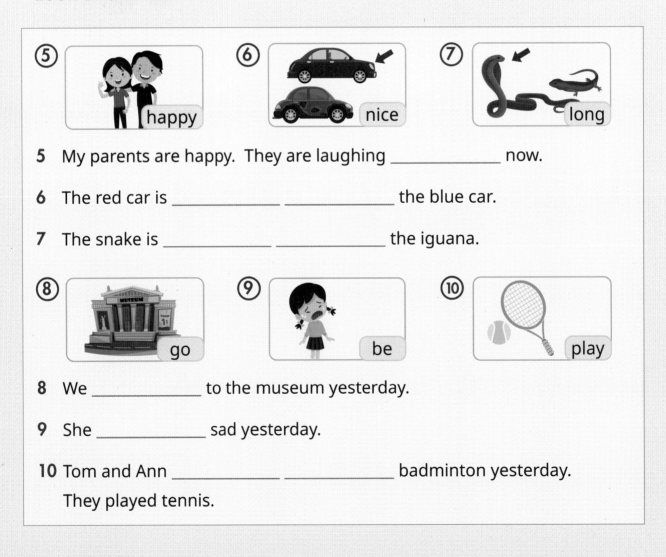

⑤ happy   ⑥ nice   ⑦ long

5 My parents are happy. They are laughing _____ now.

6 The red car is _____ _____ the blue car.

7 The snake is _____ _____ the iguana.

⑧ go   ⑨ be   ⑩ play

8 We _____ to the museum yesterday.

9 She _____ sad yesterday.

10 Tom and Ann _____ _____ badminton yesterday.
   They played tennis.

◆ Look and complete the dialogues.

11

Tom

_____ _____ they?

They are socks.

_____ socks _____ they?

They are Tom's socks.

12

study

_____ she _____ English yesterday?

Yes, she _____ .

13

take

_____ you _____ a bus yesterday?

No, I _____ .

I _____ a train.

◆ Find and correct the mistakes.

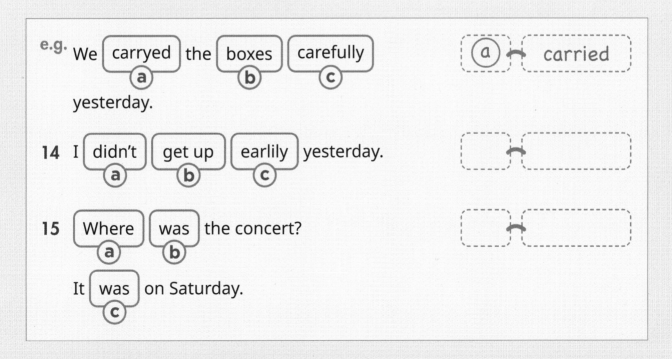

e.g. We [carryed] the [boxes] [carefully] yesterday.
      (a)   (b)   (c)

(a) ⤺ carried

14 I [didn't] [get up] [earlily] yesterday.
     (a)   (b)   (c)

_____ ⤺ _____

15 [Where] [was] the concert?
     (a)   (b)

It [was] on Saturday.
    (c)

_____ ⤺ _____

Grammar Audio Lessons

- If you need help to understand the grammar, scan the QR code using your phone.
- This will give you immediate access to detailed audio lessons in Korean.
- You can select and play each lesson from the list.

Unit 01
1. Count and Non-count Nouns
2. a/an/the + Noun

Unit 02
1. Be Verb: Positives and Negatives
2. Be Verb: Questions

Unit 03
1. There + Be + Count Noun
2. There + Be + Non-count Noun

Unit 05
1. Present Simple: Positives and Negatives
2. Regular and Irregular Verbs

Unit 06
1. Present Simple: Do you/we/they ...?
2. Present Simple: Does he/she/it ...?

Unit 07
1. Present Continuous: Positives
2. Present Continuous: Negatives

Unit 08
1. Present Continuous Question: Singular
2. Present Continuous Question: Plural

Unit 10
1. Let's
2. Imperatives

Unit 11
1. Future: Positives
2. Future: Negatives

Scope & Sequence

Unit	Grammar Point	Key Sentences	Key Vocabulary
01	Nouns and Articles (a/an/the)	He has a sandwich. The sandwich is big. They have milk. The milk is warm.	an apple, a sandwich, a knife, a woman, apples, sandwiches, knives, women, bread, butter, milk, juice, the sun, the moon
02	Present Simple: Be Verbs	Kate is a zookeeper. Kate isn't a pilot. Is Steve a pilot?	vet, zookeeper, pilot, sick, okay, old, young, bored, excited, big, small
03	There + Be + Noun	There is a carrot. There are some carrots. There is some water.	a potato, an onion, a carrot, onions, carrots, soup, cheese, water, salt
04	Review 1		
05	Present Simple: Positives and Negatives	She has breakfast at 7 o'clock. She doesn't have breakfast at 8 o'clock.	get up, walk, brush, drink, clean, study, do, play, take, have, like, catch, pass, mix, fly, carry, try
06	Present Simple: Questions	Do you get up at 7:00 every day? Does Kate watch TV at night?	get up, take, wash, go, study, watch, live, have
07	Present Continuous: Positives and Negatives	I am talking to my friend now. I'm not studying. She is sitting on a bench now. She isn't standing.	walking, standing, playing, talking, studying, riding, dancing, driving, jogging, sitting, swimming
08	Present Continuous: Questions	Are you writing a letter? Is Nate making a cake? Are they eating the cake?	studying, eating, singing, writing, making, blowing up
09	Review 2 + Mini Test 1 (Unit 01-08)		
10	Let's and Imperatives	Let's play soccer. Listen to your teacher in class. Don't run in the library.	go, play, ride, run, open, close, listen, wear, forget
11	Future: Positives and Negatives	I'll go to the hospital tomorrow. I won't go to school.	go, stay, be, watch, meet
12	Future: Questions	Will you go swimming? Will they climb a mountain? Will it be rainy tomorrow?	visit, take, go swimming, go on a trip, go shopping, climb, be
13	Review 3 + Mini Test 2 (Unit 05-12)		

Unit	Grammar Point	Key Sentences	Key Vocabulary
14	Past: Be Verbs	Amy was at the zoo yesterday. Ted and Ben weren't at the zoo. Were you bored yesterday?	at the zoo, at the museum, at the hospital, at home, at school, excited, bored, sunny
15	Past: Regular Verbs	He visited his grandma yesterday. He didn't visit his friend. They studied English. They didn't study Spanish.	walked, watched, visited, jumped, played, danced, baked, liked, practiced, studied, cried, carried, tried
16	Past: Irregular Verbs	He got up early yesterday. He didn't get up late. They went on a picnic yesterday. They didn't go fishing.	came, drank, gave, wrote, got, did, had, made, saw, took, went, ate, bought, read, cut
17	Past: Questions	Did you walk to school yesterday? Did she cook breakfast yesterday?	go, walk, do, cook, read, drink
18	Review 4 + Mini Test 3 (Unit 10-17)		
19	Wh- Question: What, Who, Whose, Where, When	Who is he? What are they? Whose cap was it? Where are the cookies? When was the test?	photo, camera, actor, photographer, ring, cap, glasses, scarf, on the table, under the bed, in March, on Thursday, at 9 o'clock
20	Adjectives and Adverbs	She is fast. She is a fast runner. She runs fast.	quiet - quietly, slow - slowly, kind - kindly, noisy - noisily, dangerous - dangerously, fast - fast, early - early, late - late, good - well
21	Comparatives	The bike is lighter than the car. The earth is bigger than the moon. The ring is more expensive than the watch.	smaller, lighter, faster, larger, nicer, bigger, hotter, heavier, easier, more expensive, more dangerous
22	Review 5 + Mini Test 4 (Unit 14-21)		

Spiral Syllabus

with 세이펜

원어민 발음을 실시간 반복학습	단어 및 예문의 우리말 해석 듣기	혼자서도 쉽게 정답 확인 가능

세이펜 핀파일 다운로드 안내

STEP ① 세이펜과 컴퓨터를 USB 케이블로 연결하세요.

STEP ② 쎄듀북 홈페이지(www.cedubook.com)에 접속 후, 학습자료실 메뉴에서 학습할 교재를 찾아 이동합니다.

> 초등교재 ▶ ELT ▶ 학습교재 클릭 ▶ 세이펜 핀파일 자료 클릭
> ▶ 다운로드 (저장을 '다른 이름으로 저장'으로 변경하여 저장소를 USB로 변경) ▶ 완료

STEP ③ 음원 다운로드가 완료되면 세이펜과 컴퓨터의 USB 케이블을 분리하세요.

STEP ④ 세이펜을 분리하면 "시스템을 초기화 중입니다. 잠시만 기다려 주세요."라는 멘트가 나옵니다.

STEP ⑤ 멘트 종료 후 세이펜을 〈Oh! My Grammar〉 표지에 대보세요.
효과음이 나온 후 바로 학습을 시작할 수 있습니다.

참고사항

◆ 세이펜은 본 교재에 포함되어 있지 않습니다. 별도로 구매하여 이용할 수 있으며, 기존에 보유하신 세이펜이 있다면 핀파일만 다운로드해서
  바로 이용하실 수 있습니다.

◆ 세이펜에서 제작된 모든 기종(기존에 보유하고 계신 기종도 호환 가능)으로 사용이 가능합니다.

◆ 모든 기종은 세이펜에서 권장하는 최신 펌웨어 업데이트를 진행해 주시기 바랍니다.
  업데이트는 세이펜 홈페이지(www.saypen.com)에서 가능합니다.

◆ 핀파일은 쎄듀북 홈페이지(www.cedubook.com)와 세이펜 홈페이지(www.saypen.com)에서 모두 다운로드 가능합니다.

◆ 세이펜을 이용하지 않는 학습자는 쎄듀북 홈페이지 부가학습자료, 교재 내 QR코드 이미지 등을 활용하여 원어민 음성으로 학습하실 수 있습니다.

◆ 기타 문의사항은 www.cedubook.com / 02-3272-4766으로 연락 바랍니다.

세이펜과 함께 배우는 Oh! My Grammar

<Oh! My Grammar>는 Student Book에 세이펜이 적용되어 있습니다.
세이펜을 영어에 가져다 대기만 하면 원어민의 생생한 영어 발음과 억양을 듣고 영어 말하기 연습을 할 수 있습니다.

*번역 기능 | 세이펜으로 책을 찍어서 원어민 음성을 들은 후, ⊤ 버튼을 짧게 누르면 해석 음원을 들을 수 있습니다.

✏️ 세이펜을 대면 유닛명을 들을 수 있습니다. ⊤ 기능 지원

✏️ QR코드에 세이펜을 대면 해당 트랙의 MP3 파일이 재생됩니다.

✏️ 세이펜을 대면 Christina 선생님의 우리말 문법 강의를 들을 수 있습니다.

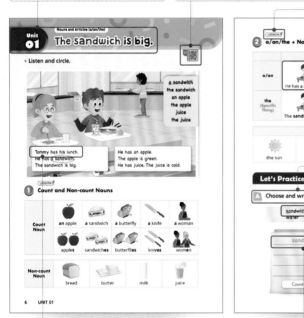

✏️ 그림이나 문장에 세이펜을 대면 원어민의 정확한 발음과 억양을 들을 수 있습니다. ⊤ 기능 지원

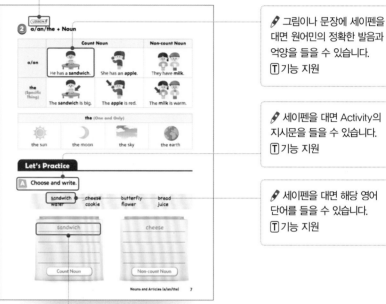

✏️ 세이펜을 대면 Activity의 지시문을 들을 수 있습니다. ⊤ 기능 지원

✏️ 세이펜을 대면 해당 영어 단어를 들을 수 있습니다. ⊤ 기능 지원

✏️ 문장에 세이펜을 대면 원어민의 정확한 발음과 억양을 들을 수 있습니다. ⊤ 기능 지원

✏️ 빈칸에 세이펜을 대면 정답을 들을 수 있습니다. ⊤ 기능 지원

✏️ 그림이나 문제에 세이펜을 대면 정답이 포함된 문장을 들을 수 있습니다. ⊤ 기능 지원

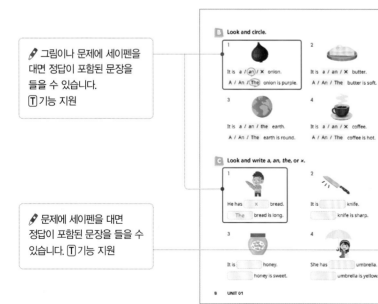

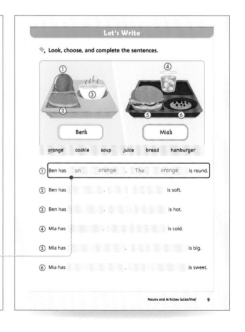

✏️ 문제에 세이펜을 대면 정답이 포함된 문장을 들을 수 있습니다. ⊤ 기능 지원

Oh! My Grammar 3

3

Workbook

CEDU BOOK

Oh! My Grammar 3

Workbook

CEDU BOOK

Contents

Nouns & Be Verbs

Present Simple & Present Continuous

Imperatives & Future Tense

Past Tense

Wh- Questions & Others

Unit 01

The sandwich is big.

Step 1 Read and write *a*, *an*, or *x*. Then, match.

1 I have ___an___ apple.   •

2 It is _____ bread.   •

3 It is _____ butterfly.   •

4 It is _____ milk.   •

5 She has _____ egg.   •

• The milk is cold.

• The butterfly is pretty.

• The egg is white.

• The bread is soft.

• The apple is green.

Step 2 Choose, circle, and write.

~~cookie~~   moon   coffee   onion

1   It is ___a cookie___. ___The cookie___ is sweet.
   (a) / an / ×   A / An / (The)

2   She has _____. _____ is hot.
   a / an / ×   A / An / The

3   Look at _____. _____ is big.
   a / an / the   A / An / The

4   He has _____. _____ is purple.
   a / an / ×   A / An / The

4   UNIT 01

Unscramble and write the sentences.

1

. It is knife a

→ It is a knife.

The sharp is . knife

→ _____

2

has bread Kevin .

→ _____

is bread The long .

→ _____

3

umbrella an has . She

→ _____

umbrella yellow is The .

→ _____

4

. The beautiful earth is

→ _____

They are vets.

Step 1 **Look and write.**

1 Emily ____is____ a zookeeper. She ____isn't____ a pilot.

2 Nate and I _____ young. We _____ old.

3 It _____ a penguin. It _____ an owl.

4 The children _____ excited. They _____ bored.

Step 2 **Look and complete the dialogues.**

1

____Is____ the woman a baker?

____No____, ____she____ ____isn't____.

2

_____ the apples red?

_____, _____ _____.

3

_____ the orange book thick?

_____, _____ _____.

4

_____ you and Alice firefighters?

_____, _____ _____.

Step 3 Unscramble and write the sentences.

1 | they | police officers | ? | Are

→ <u>Are they police officers?</u>

2 | angry | . | The girl | is

→ _____

3 | the backpack | new | ? | Is

→ _____

4 | Luke and Amy | doctors | Are | ?

→ _____

5 | a writer | . | not | The man | is

→ _____

6 | are | . | sad | not | We

→ _____

Unit 03

There is some cheese.

Read and write _There is_ or _There are_.

1 ___There___ ___are___ lemons.

2 _____ _____ a potato.

3 _____ _____ some grapes.

4 _____ _____ salt.

5 _____ _____ strawberries.

6 _____ _____ some water.

Step 2 **Look and write with _a_, _an_, or _some_.**

1
carrot

There ___is___ ___a___ ___carrot___.

2
cheese

There _____ _____ _____.

3
onion

There _____ _____ _____.

4
eggs

There _____ _____ _____.

Unscramble and write the sentences.

1

is . watermelon There a

→ There is a watermelon.

2

milk is There some .

→

3

cups There some . are

→

4

There orange is . an

→

5

some . There jam is

→

6

some There . are sandwiches

→

Step 1 Look and write *a*, *an*, *the*, or *some*.

1

I have _____*a*_____ tomato.

_____The_____ tomato is red.

2

Look at _____ sky.

_____ moon is beautiful.

3

There is _____ egg.

_____ egg is white.

4

There is _____ soup.

_____ soup is hot.

Step 2 Look and write.

1 They _____are_____ vets.

They _____aren't_____ zookeepers.

2 There _____ a dog.

3 There _____ some cats.

4 The dog _____ big.

It _____ small.

5 _____ the dog sick?

Yes, _____ _____.

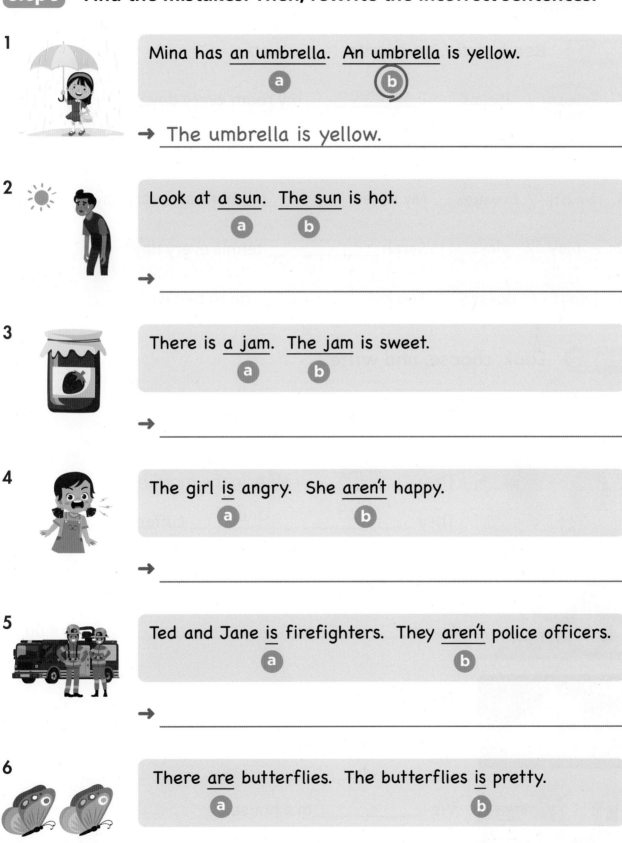

Step 3 ▸ **Find the mistakes. Then, rewrite the incorrect sentences.**

1

Mina has <u>an umbrella</u>. <u>An umbrella</u> is yellow.
ⓐ   ⓑ

➜ The umbrella is yellow.

2

Look at <u>a sun</u>. <u>The sun</u> is hot.
ⓐ   ⓑ

➜ _____

3

There is <u>a jam</u>. <u>The jam</u> is sweet.
ⓐ   ⓑ

➜ _____

4

The girl <u>is</u> angry. She <u>aren't</u> happy.
ⓐ   ⓑ

➜ _____

5

Ted and Jane <u>is</u> firefighters. They <u>aren't</u> police officers.
ⓐ   ⓑ

➜ _____

6

There <u>are</u> butterflies. The butterflies <u>is</u> pretty.
ⓐ   ⓑ

➜ _____

Unit 05

Mia studies English.

Step 1 Read, circle, and write.

1 (clean) / cleans   I _____clean_____ my room every day.

2 don't / doesn't   We _____ like hamburgers.

3 brush / brushes   My sister _____ her hair every day.

4 play / plays   Sarah _____ tennis every day.

5 don't / doesn't   The kid _____ go to bed early.

Step 2 Look, choose, and write.

drink	have	get up	live

They ____drink____ coffee in the morning.

They ____don't____ ____drink____ coffee at night.

Mina _____ _____ at 7:00.

She _____ _____ _____ at 8:00.

The boy _____ a puppy.

He _____ _____ a kitten.

We _____ in a house.

We _____ _____ in an apartment.

Change the sentences.

1

I go swimming on Thursday.

→ He _goes swimming on Thursday._____

2

Emily doesn't study on Sunday.

→ Emily and Steve _____

3

We don't play soccer on Monday.

→ Oliver _____

4

I fix the computer.

→ My brother _____

5

The student doesn't walk to school.

→ They _____

6

The plane flies in the sky.

→ The birds _____

7

My sister and I have breakfast every day.

→ My dad _____

Unit 06

Does he get up early?

Step 1 **Read and write.**

1 [Do] you go to a park on Saturday?   Yes, [I] [do].

2 [　　] the girl get up early every day?   No, [　　] [　　].

3 [　　] a giraffe have a long neck?   Yes, [　　] [　　].

4 [　　] Sam and Steve live in the city?   No, [　　] [　　].

Step 2 **Look and complete the dialogues.**

1
Friday

_____Do_____ you watch a movie on Friday?

_____Yes_____, ____we____ ____do____.

2

_____ your dad help with your homework?

_____, _____ _____.

3
Sunday

_____ they go shopping on Sunday?

_____, _____ _____.

4
7:00 a.m.

_____ she wash her face at 8:00?

_____, _____ _____.

Step 3 ▸ **Change the sentences to questions.**

1 You take a shower every day.

   → <u>Do you take a shower every day?</u>

2 A rabbit has long ears.

   → _____

3 Sandy goes to bed at 10 o'clock.

   → _____

4 They watch TV every day.

   → _____

5 Aaron studies math in the evening.

   → _____

6 Kate and Tom ride bikes every day.

   → _____

Unit 07

I am riding a bike.

Step 1 Read and write.

1 **help**

    I ____am____ ____helping____ my mom now.

2 **not / sing**

    The birds _____ _____ now.

3 **not / take**

    He _____ _____ a shower now.

4 **swim**

    The dolphin _____ _____ in the sea now.

Step 2 Look, choose, and write.

~~talk~~	drive	sit	jog

1

    I ____am____ ____talking____ to my friend now.

    I ____am____ ____not____ ____talking____ to my teacher.

2

    The children _____ _____ in the park now.

    They _____ _____ on the playground.

3

    Susan _____ _____ on a bench now.

    She _____ _____ on the grass.

4

    The man _____ _____ a car now.

    He _____ _____ a truck.

Step 3 Unscramble and write the sentences.

1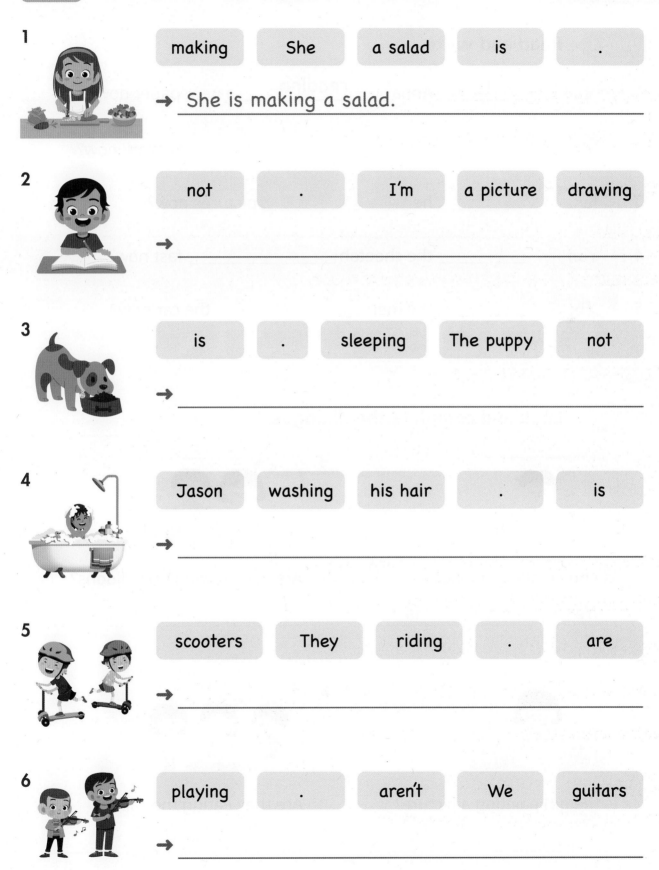

| making | She | a salad | is | . |

→ She is making a salad.

2

| not | . | I'm | a picture | drawing |

→ _____

3

| is | . | sleeping | The puppy | not |

→ _____

4

| Jason | washing | his hair | . | is |

→ _____

5

| scooters | They | riding | . | are |

→ _____

6

| playing | . | aren't | We | guitars |

→ _____

Unit 08 Are you studying?

Step 1 Read and write.

1 read _____Is_____ Anna _____reading_____ a newspaper now?

2 do _____ you _____ your homework now?

3 take _____ he _____ pictures now?

4 run _____ the cheetah _____ fast now?

5 fix _____ the men _____ the car now?

Step 2 Look and complete the dialogues.

1

Is Andy making cookies?

_____Yes_____ , _____he_____ _____is_____.

2

Are you blowing up balloons?

_____, _____ _____.

3

Is the girl painting a picture?

_____, _____ _____.

4

Are they eating the cake?

_____, _____ _____.

1

Q Are you eating ice cream? _____

eating / Are / ice cream / you / ?

A Yes, ____I____ ____am____.

2

Q _____

Sam / ? / Is / dancing

A No, _____ _____.

3

Q _____

she / ? / the ball / catching / Is

A Yes, _____ _____.

4

Q _____

? / Are / jumping / the rabbits

A Yes, _____ _____.

5

Q _____

raining / Is / it / ?

A Yes, _____ _____.

6

Q _____

Are / the dishes / ? / they / doing

A No, _____ _____.

Review 2

Step 1 **Read, circle, and match.**

1 Is Tina rideing / (riding) a bike now? . . . . | Yes, it does. |

2 Do / Does a zebra have stripes? | Yes, I am. |

3 Are / Do you walking the dog now? | No, I don't. |

4 Are / Do you watch TV every day? | No, she isn't. |

5 Are the kids runing / running now? | Yes, they are. |

Step 2 **Look and write the correct forms of the verbs.**

1
   eat

   We ___are___ ___eating___ ice cream now.

   We ___aren't___ ___eating___ chocolate.

2
   cut

   I _____ _____ carrots now.

   I _____ _____ _____ onions.

3  Sunday
   wash

   Annie _____ the dog on Sunday.

   She _____ _____ the car.

4  2:00 p.m.
   study

   The boy _____ math at 2:00.

   He _____ _____ English at 2:00.

Unscramble and write the sentences.

1

washes   He   every day   his hair   .

→ He washes his hair every day.

2

are   .   The rabbits   jumping

→ _____

3

you   ?   writing   in your diary   Are

→ _____

4

doesn't   in the city   My grandpa   .   live

→ _____

5

isn't   Jenny   basketball   .   playing

→ _____

6

Do   every day   ?   take a walk   they

→ _____

Unit 10
Let's go outside.

Step 1 ▶ **Read and write with *Let's* or *Let's not*.**

1 ride It's cold outside. ____Let's not ride____ a bike.

2 have I'm hungry. _____ spaghetti.

3 play It's raining outside. _____ outside.

4 make Today is Dad's birthday. _____ a cake.

5 go We have a test tomorrow. _____ to a movie.

Step 2 ▶ **Look and write.**

1

drink

____Don't drink____ soda.

____Drink____ some water.

2
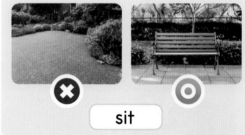
sit

_____ on the grass.

_____ on the bench.

3

read

_____ a comic book.

_____ a newspaper.

4

eat

_____ ice cream.

_____ an apple.

Unscramble and write the sentences.

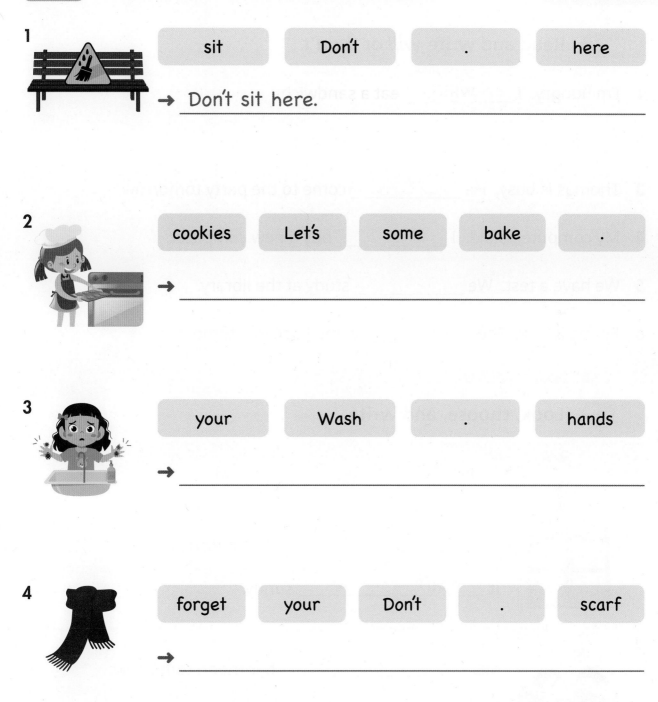

1. sit | Don't | . | here
→ Don't sit here.

2. cookies | Let's | some | bake | .
→ _____

3. your | Wash | . | hands
→ _____

4. forget | your | Don't | . | scarf
→ _____

5. it | . | not | Let's | eat
→ _____

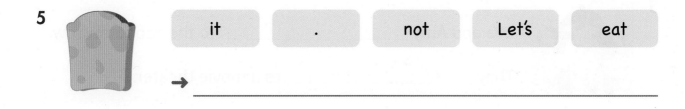

Unit 11

I will go to the hospital.

Step 1 **Read and write *will* or *won't*.**

1 I'm hungry. I _____will_____ eat a sandwich.

2 The sky is gray. It _____ rain soon.

3 Thomas is busy. He _____ come to the party tomorrow.

4 My computer is old. I _____ buy a new computer.

5 We have a test. We _____ study at the library.

6 Emma is sick. She _____ come to school tomorrow.

Step 2 **Look, choose, and write.**

be	go	meet

1

It ____will____ ____be____ rainy tomorrow.

It ____won't____ ____be____ sunny.

2

Mia _____ _____ her friend tomorrow.

She _____ _____ her grandparents.

3

Mia and Amy _____ _____ to the zoo tomorrow.

They _____ _____ to a movie theater.

Unscramble and write the sentences.

1
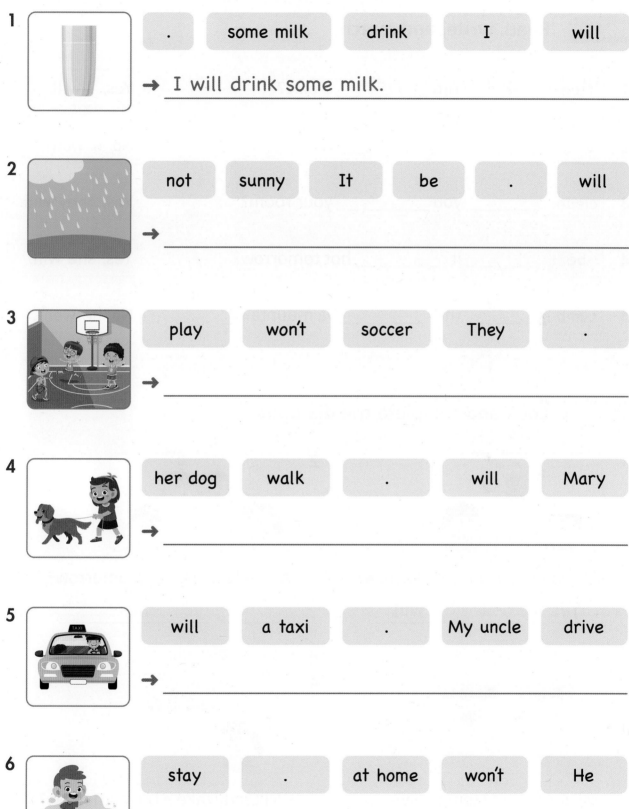

| . | some milk | drink | I | will |

→ I will drink some milk.

2

| not | sunny | It | be | . | will |

→ _____

3

| play | won't | soccer | They | . |

→ _____

4

| her dog | walk | . | will | Mary |

→ _____

5

| will | a taxi | . | My uncle | drive |

→ _____

6

| stay | . | at home | won't | He |

→ _____

Unit 12   Will you go swimming?

Step 1 **Read, write, and match.**

1   ride   ___Will___ Tim ___ride___ a bike? ....   Yes, I will.

2   stay   _____ Amy _____ at a hotel?   No, it won't.

3   clean   _____ you _____ your room?   Yes, they will.

4   be   _____ it _____ hot tomorrow?   Yes, she will.

5   climb   _____ they _____ a mountain?   No, he won't.

Step 2 **Look and complete the dialogues.**

1

Will you go on a trip tomorrow?

___Yes___, ___I___ ___will___.

2

Will they go skating tomorrow?

_____, _____ _____.

3

Will it be sunny tomorrow?

_____, _____ _____.

4

Will Cindy take a bus tomorrow?

_____, _____ _____.

Step 3 **Unscramble and write the questions.**

1.
| early | Will | get up | he |

Q Will he get up early _____ tomorrow?

A Yes, he will.

2.
| Helen | Will | her friend | meet |

Q _____ tomorrow?

A No, she won't.

3.
| you | swimming | Will | go |

Q _____ tomorrow?

A No, we won't.

4.
| Will | to the beach | they | go |

Q _____ tomorrow?

A Yes, they will.

5.
| be | Will | it | snowy |

Q _____ tomorrow?

A Yes, it will.

6.
| walk | you | Will | to school |

Q _____ tomorrow?

A No, I won't.

Step 1 **Look and write with *Let's* or *Let's not*.**

①  wash ②  play ③  eat ④  help

1 __Let's wash__ the dishes. 2 _____ outside.

3 _____ the bread. 4 _____ the boy.

Step 2 **Look and write the correct forms of the verbs.**

1  eat

__Don't__ __eat__ fast food.

__Eat__ healthy food.

2  drink

_____ _____ soda.

_____ some water.

3  go

_____ you _____ on a trip tomorrow?

Yes, _____ _____.

4 clean

_____ they _____ the classroom tomorrow?

No, _____ _____.

They _____ _____ the park.

Unscramble and write the sentences.

1. coat | Wear | your | .

    → Wear your coat.

2. forget | Do | your scarf | not | .

    → _____

3. will | tomorrow | go fishing | We | .

    → _____

4. cookies | some | bake | Let's | .

    → _____

5. My brother | stay | . | won't | at home

    → _____

6. be | Will | ? | sunny | it

    → _____

Unit 14 Amy was at the zoo.

Step 1 **Read and write.**

Today	Yesterday
We are at the theater.	1 We ___were___ at the theater.
The movie isn't funny.	2 The movie _____ funny.
The cat is hungry.	3 The cat _____ hungry.
My mother is angry.	4 My mother _____ angry.
They aren't at the pool.	5 They _____ at the pool.
The students are at the zoo.	6 The students _____ at the zoo.

Step 2 **Look and write in the past tense.**

1

Liam ___was___ at the hospital.

He ___wasn't___ at home.

2

We _____ at the museum.

We _____ at school.

3

_____ Ted excited yesterday?

Yes, _____ _____.

_____ Lily excited yesterday?

No, _____ _____.

4

_____ it sunny yesterday?

No, _____ _____.

_____ you bored yesterday?

Yes, _____ _____.

Unscramble and write the sentences.

1 . yesterday was He at the playground

→ He was at the playground yesterday.

2 yesterday weren't . We tired

→ _____

3 . were They late yesterday

→ _____

4 wasn't at school I . yesterday

→ _____

5 you Were ? yesterday at the farm

→ _____

6 yesterday ? rainy Was it

→ _____

Unit 15 I watched a concert.

Step 1 Read, circle, and write.

1 We ___finished___ our homework yesterday.

finishd / (finished)

2 She _____ volleyball yesterday.

played / plaied

3 The children _____ the park yesterday.

cleand / cleaned

4 Susan _____ the movie yesterday.

liked / likeed

5 My brother _____ loudly yesterday.

cryed / cried

Step 2 Look and write.

①
watch

②
visit

③
study

④
practice

1 They ___watched___ a soccer game yesterday.

They ___didn't___ ___watch___ a movie.

2 Andy _____ his grandma yesterday.

He _____ _____ his friend.

3 Henry and I _____ English yesterday.

We _____ _____ French.

4 He _____ the piano yesterday.

He _____ _____ the violin.

Change the sentences into the past tense.

1   She doesn't walk to school.

→ _She didn't walk to school_ _____ yesterday.

2   They carry the heavy boxes.

→ _____ yesterday.

3   We don't watch the soccer game.

→ _____ yesterday.

4   Lucy helps the teacher.

→ _____ yesterday.

5   It doesn't rain.

→ _____ yesterday.

6   Kevin doesn't wash his car.

→ _____ yesterday.

7   My mom and I bake cookies.

→ _____ yesterday.

Unit 16

I drank soda.

Step 1 **Read and write.**

1 | come | Chloe _____came_____ to my house yesterday.

2 | eat | The horse _____ some carrots yesterday.

3 | read | My uncle _____ a newspaper yesterday.

4 | write | I _____ an email yesterday.

5 | see | They _____ Mr. Green yesterday.

Step 2 **Look and write.**

①
get up

②
go

③
buy

④
make

1 I _____got_____ _____up_____ early yesterday.

I _____didn't_____ _____get_____ _____up_____ late.

2 We _____ to the park yesterday.

We _____ _____ to the zoo.

3 Amy _____ apples yesterday.

She _____ _____ oranges.

4 Amy and Tom _____ an apple pie yesterday.

They _____ _____ a cake.

Unscramble and write the sentences.

1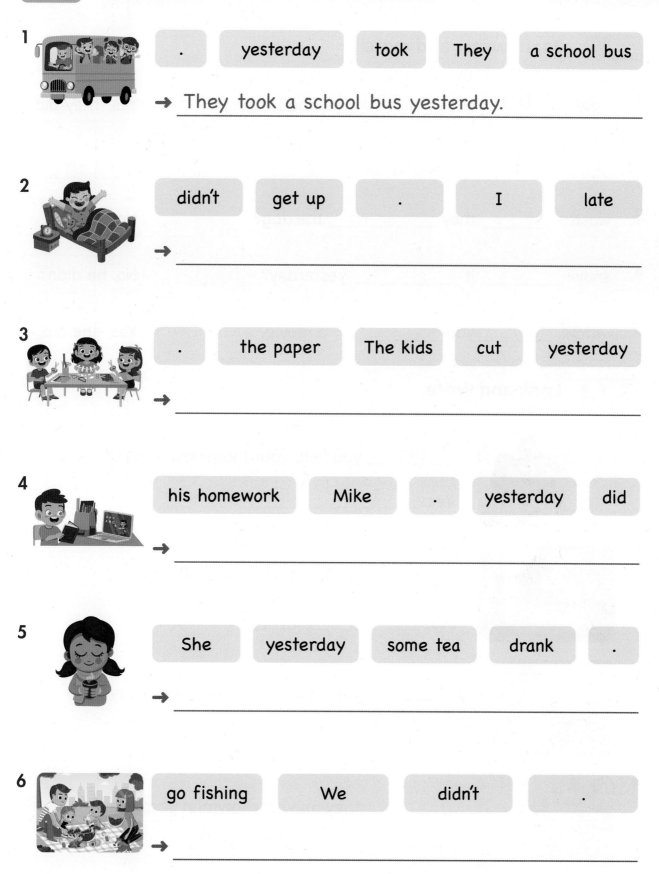

| . | yesterday | took | They | a school bus |

→ They took a school bus yesterday.

2

| didn't | get up | . | I | late |

→ _____

3

| . | the paper | The kids | cut | yesterday |

→ _____

4

| his homework | Mike | . | yesterday | did |

→ _____

5

| She | yesterday | some tea | drank | . |

→ _____

6

| go fishing | We | didn't | . |

→ _____

Unit 17 Did you go to bed late?

Step 1 **Read, write, and match.**

1 go   ___Did___ she ___go___ to bed late? ········· Yes, they did.

2 take   _____ Eric _____ the subway? Yes, I did.

3 wash   _____ they _____ the dog? No, it didn't.

4 snow   _____ it _____ yesterday? No, he didn't.

5 watch   _____ you _____ a movie? Yes, she did.

Step 2 **Look and write.**

1
___Did___ you help your mom yesterday?

Yes, ___I___ ___did___.

2
_____ Susan study at the library?

No, _____ _____.

3
_____ your dad read a book yesterday?

No, _____ _____.

4
_____ they make a snowman yesterday?

Yes, _____ _____.

Unscramble and write the questions.

1

| it | ? | rain | yesterday | Did |

Q Did it rain yesterday?

A Yes, it did.

2

| Did | the drums | play | ? | she |

Q _____

A Yes, she did.

3

| a salad | Did | ? | have | Peter |

Q _____

A No, he didn't.

4

| late | get up | Did | you | ? |

Q _____

A No, I didn't.

5

| you | eat | ? | ice cream | Did |

Q _____

A Yes, we did.

6

| ? | stay | at home | they | Did |

Q _____

A No, they didn't.

Step 1 **Look, choose, and write.**

①  ②  ③  ④

| ~~be~~ | read | make | practice |

1 They _____ were _____ at school yesterday.

2 I _____ yoga yesterday.

3 She _____ cookies yesterday.

4 Thomas _____ a book yesterday.

Step 2 **Look and write.**

1  be

_____ Was _____ Luna excited yesterday?

Yes, she _____ was _____.

2  be

_____ you at home yesterday?

No, we _____. We _____ at the farm.

3  go

_____ they _____ camping yesterday?

No, they _____. They _____ shopping.

4  study

_____ he _____ math yesterday?

Yes, he _____.

Step 3 Correct the mistakes and rewrite.

1 My sister <u>cryed</u> yesterday.

→ My sister cried yesterday.

2 We <u>was</u> tired yesterday.

→ _____

3 I <u>am</u> at the bookstore yesterday.

→ _____

4 The monkey <u>eated</u> the banana yesterday.

→ _____

5 <u>Do</u> you visit your grandparents yesterday?

→ _____

6 Mark <u>didn't finished</u> his homework yesterday.

→ _____

7 <u>Was</u> the students at the zoo yesterday?

→ _____

Where were you?

Step 1 **Read, circle, and write.**

1 When / (Where)   ___Where___ was your cap?

It was under the chair.

2 Who / Whose   _____ coat is it?

It is Erin's coat.

3 When / Where   _____ is the magic show?

It is on Saturday.

4 Who / What   _____ were the children?

They were my classmates.

Step 2 **Look and complete the dialogues.**

  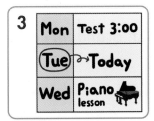 

1 ___What___ ___are___ they?   They are cameras.

2 _____ _____ the cookies?   They were in the jar.

3 _____ _____ the test?   It was at 3 o'clock.

4 _____ _____ _____ it?   It is Megan's scarf.

1

| was | When | your birthday | ? |

Q When was your birthday?

A It was in April.

2

| the English test | When | ? | is |

Q _____

A It is at 4 o'clock.

3

| the man | Who | was | ? |

Q _____

A He was my uncle.

4

| are | Whose | ? | they | mittens |

Q _____

A They are Steve's mittens.

5

| Where | ? | was | your baseball |

Q _____

A It was under the bed.

6

| is | ? | it | umbrella | Whose |

Q _____

A It is Gina's umbrella.

Unit 20　She speaks quietly.

Step 1 Look and write the *adjectives* and *adverbs*.

1
slow

The man is a ___slow___ walker.

He walks ___slowly___.

2
careful

The woman is a _____ driver.

She drives the car _____.

3
fast

Clara is a _____ runner.

She runs _____.

4
good

Mike is a _____ soccer player.

He plays soccer _____.

Step 2 Correct the mistakes.

1 Ms. Lee was a <u>kindly</u> doctor. → kind

2 They are <u>well</u> pianists. →

3 My brother woke up <u>lately</u>. →

4 A lion is a <u>dangerously</u> animal. →

5 Students talk <u>quiet</u> in the library. →

6 Kate and Anna are talking <u>happyly</u>. →

1

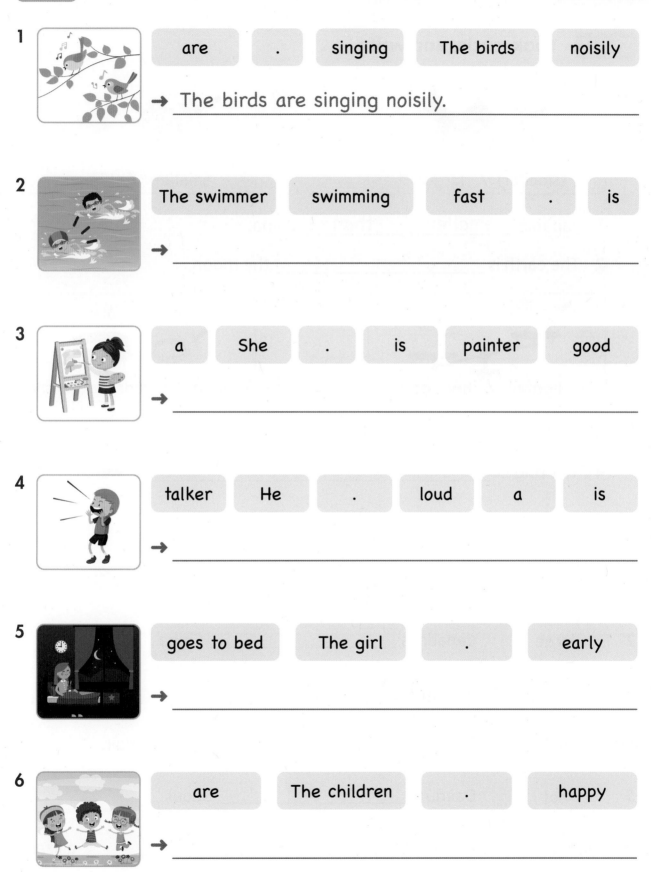

| are | . | singing | The birds | noisily |

→ The birds are singing noisily.

2

| The swimmer | swimming | fast | . | is |

→ _____

3

| a | She | . | is | painter | good |

→ _____

4

| talker | He | . | loud | a | is |

→ _____

5

| goes to bed | The girl | . | early |

→ _____

6

| are | The children | . | happy |

→ _____

Unit 21 The car is faster than the bike.

Step 1 Look, circle, and write.

①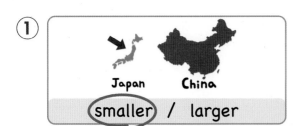

1 Japan is __smaller__ __than__ China.

2 The earth is _____ _____ the moon.

②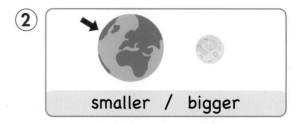

③

3 The zebra is _____ _____ the hippo.

4 The ring is _____ _____ _____ the watch.

④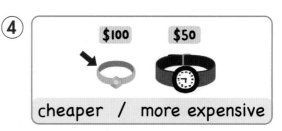

Step 2 Read and write.

1 old My dad is __older__ __than__ my mom.

2 large Canada is _____ _____ China.

3 heavy An egg is _____ _____ water.

4 short Sam's hair is _____ _____ Lina's hair.

5 hot Daegu is _____ _____ Seoul.

6 dangerous An alligator is _____ _____ _____ a lizard.

Unscramble and write the sentences.

1

| a cat | . | A tiger | is | than | bigger |

→ A tiger is bigger than a cat.

2

| than | a car | A train | faster | . | is |

→

3

| is | the blue car | . | than | The red car | nicer |

→

4

| is | A basketball | than | . | heavier | a tennis ball |

→

5

| shorter | my dad | My brother | is | . | than |

→

6

| is | more expensive | The camera | . | the book | than |

→

Review 5

Step 1 **Read, circle, and write.**

1 (kind) / kindly   Ms. Steven is a ____kind____ teacher.

2 good / well   Lucas can speak Korean _____.

3 quiet / quietly   The students are _____ in the library.

4 Who / Whose   _____ cap was it?   It was David's cap.

5 Who / What   _____ is the girl?   She is my cousin.

6 When / Where   _____ was the key?   It was under the sofa.

Step 2 **Look, choose, and write.**

| slow | expensive | large | light |

1   A bike is ___slower___ ___than___ a car.

2   The sun is _____ _____ the moon.

3   An apple is _____ _____ a watermelon.

4   The dress is _____ _____ _____ the skirt.

Unscramble and write the sentences.

1 | late | | came | | The school bus | | . |

→ The school bus came late.

2 | is | heavier | . | a mouse | than | An elephant |

→ _____

3 | cheaper | The bike | . | the car | is | than |

→ _____

4 | is | . | The woman | pianist | a | good |

→ _____

5 | ? | When | the English test | was |

→ Q _____

A It was on Tuesday.

6 | they | Whose | are | ? | glasses |

→ Q _____

A They are my teacher's glasses.

Oh! My Grammar is a three-level grammar series designed for young students. *Oh! My Grammar* helps learners to easily understand basic grammar form, use, and meaning while also developing their writing skills. This series exposes students to natural English grammar so that they can learn how to use it in real-life situations. Learner-centered exercises enable students to use the grammar forms accurately and fluently. Interesting writing tasks and gradual sentence pattern practice boost students' confidence in their writing skills.

Oh! My Grammar Series

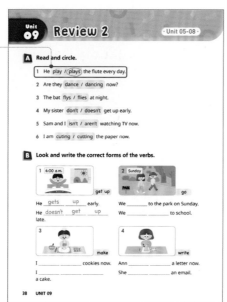

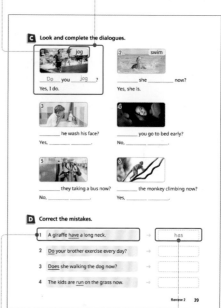

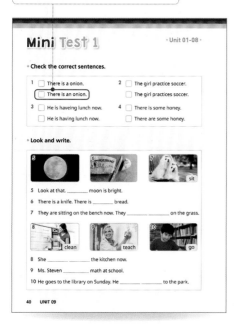

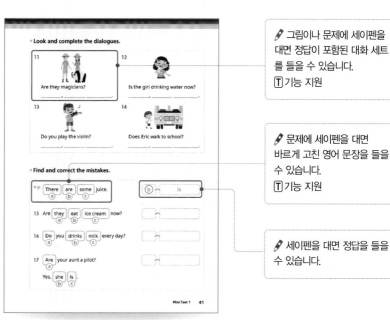

초등코치 천일문과 세이펜의 만남!

SAYPEN
www.saypen.com

초등코치 천일문 시리즈 ✕ 세이펜 학습의 장점

01	02	03	04	05
녹음기능을 활용하여 발음 교정 및 쉐도잉 학습 가능	112개 대표 패턴 및 모든 문장을 원어민 발음으로 실시간 재생	게임모드를 활용한 즐거운 영어학습 가능	Role play를 이용한 가상 대화 체험 (Sentence에 한함)	이해하기 어려운 문법적 내용을 쉬운 해설과 함께 바로듣기 가능 (Grammar에 한함)

* 〈초등코치 천일문 시리즈〉는 세이펜이 적용된 도서입니다.
  세이펜을 영어에 가져다 대기만 하면 원어민이 들려주는 생생한 영어 발음과 억양을 바로 확인할 수 있습니다.

* 세이펜은 본 교재에 포함되어 있지 않습니다. 기존에 보유하신 세이펜이 있다면 핀파일만 다운로드해서 바로 이용하실 수 있습니다.
  단, Role-Play 기능은 SBS-1000 이후 모델에서만 구동됩니다.